UNIVERSALISM: FACT OR FICTION

EXAMINING WHAT SCRIPTURE SAYS ABOUT THE SCOPE OF SALVATION

DALE HILL

TWS PUBLISHING

Published by TWS Publishing
Lodi, CA
www.thewriterssocietypublishing.com

Paperback ISBN: 978-1-966818-44-1

Kindle ISBN: 978-1-966818-45-8

CONTENTS

ENDORSEMENTS

With *Universalism: Fact or Fiction*, readers are offered a substantive and well-documented contribution to the study of Christian eschatology. Dale Hill skillfully navigates biblical interpretation, patristic theology, and doctrinal development with commendable breadth, situating the conversation about apokatastasis within its proper historical and exegetical contexts, without neglecting the still-speaking voice of the Spirit. By challenging inherited paradigms with careful arguments and robust engagement with sources, this volume will serve as a valuable resource for scholars, ministers, and students seeking to engage critically with the only doctrine that is as maligned as it is misunderstood: universal salvation.

MATTHEW B. PANDEL, PH.D., TH.D.
PRESIDENT AND PROFESSOR OF TRINITARIAN THEOLOGY
GLOBAL GRACE SEMINARY

Finally, we have a well-researched book that takes an honest look at the three major theologies we are faced with today. The author does a great job laying out Calvinism, Arminianism, and Universalism. The book honestly explores all three with supporting Scriptures and legitimate objections. This gem pulls no punches and takes head-on each of the three. It was informative, easy to read, and brought to the table points I had not considered. I think the book would be a great small group study guide, leading to honest and open discussion. I highly recommend it and encourage you to pick up two copies—one for yourself and one to give away. I guarantee you that you will not be disappointed.

DON KEATHLEY
FOUNDER OF GLOBAL GRACE SEMINARY
FOUNDER OF THE GRACE AWAKENING TELEVISION NETWORK

Dale Hill has masterfully explored the doctrine of universal salvation with both depth and clarity. He builds a strong case on the biblical foundations of Christian Universalism while thoughtfully addressing the objections often raised when this topic arises. With boldness and precision, Dale dives deep into Scripture—bringing out its contextual meanings and answering the questions many are hesitant to ask. What stands out is his fearless and thorough approach. Rather than shying away from difficult passages, Dale engages them head-on, helping readers see Jesus' universal act of redemption in a new light. Whether you are just beginning to explore this doctrine or have been studying it for years, this book will stretch you, challenge you, and grow your understanding of the universal salvation accomplished in Christ. This is not only a book to read, but one that invites discussion and reflection—making it an excellent choice for a group study.

LISA WENTWORTH COUTURE, AUTHOR

Reading Dale Hill's book *UNIVERSALISM: Fact or Fiction* reminded me of something I did as a teacher. I completed a yearly exercise of creating a "Scope and Sequence" chart in which I laid out the "scope" of the curriculum that would be taught and the "sequence" in which said curriculum was to be presented. This is what Dale has done for those "students" of Scripture who would humbly set aside preconceived notions of the meaning of universalism.

Step-by-step, the reader is invited to mine not only Scripture but also explore language and culture and begin to take an honest look at, and perhaps even question, what has been presented as the good news of the gospel of Jesus.

Challenging? Yes! But Dale patiently and lovingly presents the case for universalism that, to my mind, is a gospel that is "good news to the poor...proclaim[ing] freedom for the prisoners and recovery of sight for the blind, [setting] the oppressed free." (Luke 4:18)

Barry Grecu
Founder, Director, Emmaus Ministries, Atlanta, GA

FOREWORD

When I read through this manuscript, what struck me wasn't just the theology—it was the heart behind it. Dale hasn't written a dry outline of Calvinism, Arminianism, and Universalism.

He's opened a window into the wideness of God's grace.

I love that he uses the word Inclusionist. That says so much. It's hopeful, it's honest, and it points right to the reality of Christ's finished work. I also love the way he shares his journey—how he's walked through different theological camps and finally found language that reflects what he's come to see in Jesus. Not labels, not boxes, just words like Hopeful Universalist and Inclusionist that describe what's already true: the cross of Jesus really did include all of humanity.

This isn't a book that argues for the sake of winning. It's a book that invites you to slow down, listen, and maybe let your thinking stretch. That's what good theology does —it shakes us free from limited beliefs and points us back to Jesus.

My prayer is that these pages stir up fresh confidence in His love and expand not only your understanding but your experience of grace plus nothing. Or in Dale's words: "grace touches everything we think, say, and do in our lives. There is no aspect of our life with which grace is not concerned."

Robin Smit, ThD
Author, Teacher, and Founder of TWS Publishing

PREFACE

I was brought into the things of the Lord in 1969. A lot was going on during those days, especially within the realm of the Spirit. Through quite a few circumstances and events, I found myself learning to teach.

The Lord anointed those early years when I knew so little, yet shared so eagerly what I did know.

In 1972, I ended up in Springfield, Missouri, at a small Bible teaching center led by Bill Britton. I learned from attending the classes, but I also learned from the fellowship, which was rich and formative.

One of the students there, who had been brought up in the Assembly of God denomination, was beginning to think in terms of what was known then as Ultimate Reconciliation.

I loved that brother dearly, and I cried deeply the day he died. I never fully bought into his ideas at the time. We would often meet over the years and would find our friendship only growing deeper. Sometimes we would be up until 2:00 or 3:00 in the morning discussing things from the Bible.

After I completed my studies in New Testament Greek, he would often check with me on a passage he was considering—just to bounce his ideas off me and see if they stacked up with my understanding of the Greek. Sometimes what he was seeing didn't make sense to me, but often it did.

But I still could not buy the concept of the eventual salvation of all mankind. At that time, I would say that I was mostly in the camp of the Arminians. This theology believes that it is up to you to choose Jesus in order to be saved, and if you walk away from Him, you might go to hell.

I hadn't been trained that way specifically, because I was brought up Catholic. In that tradition, at that time, you had to be a Catholic to be saved, but heaven still was not a guarantee. Purgatory was most likely your first stop after death.

It was learning the Greek language of the New Testament that began to change my theology. Yes, there are many of the Arminian school of thought who are scholars and have much more Greek than I will ever hope to know. So, I don't mean to imply that those of that persuasion are less than educated.

However, the commentaries I was introduced to—and the study aids available to the student who knows just enough Greek to be dangerous (me)—began to open my mind to the teachings of John Calvin.

Much more of the Scriptures began to make sense to me within this line of thought. I have "traveled" with this school for almost 40 years. I bought into the TULIP way of thinking about our salvation.

For those of you who may not be familiar, TULIP is an acronym for the Five Points of Calvinism, which form the basis of their systematic theology.

In its brief form—

T = total depravity of the human
U = unconditional election by God to salvation
L = limited atonement in the death of Jesus
I = irresistible grace for salvation
P = perseverance of the saints, so as to never lose their salvation

There are plenty of Scripture verses for each of these concepts—
except one: limited atonement. Limited atonement means that Jesus
died only for the elect, not for others. The weakness in this for me
was that it is based more on a logical progression of thought than
on Scripture.

Yes, it makes sense if it is true that there are only certain ones whom
God has chosen for salvation. However, that kind of thinking began
to bother me.

Then, sometime in 2018, I began to listen to a teacher named Don
Keathley. I enjoyed the way he opened the Scriptures for his
congregation and for those of us who found him online. But then I
began to realize he was teaching things related to universalism, and
I just could not cope with that.

I quit following him.

But when the Lord wants you to know something, you cannot get
away from His persistence. It was called irresistible grace in my
camp.

Now, here I am today, at the end of 2022, very much a follower of
Don Keathley. I listen to him on Wednesday nights, and I catch his
Sunday live message later on in the day via recording. I have also
graduated with a Master's in Theology from Global Grace
Seminary, of which he is the president.

WHAT CHANGED?

I have been a student of the Bible since the early 1970s. God gave me a love for His written Word, and I have never lost it. Admittedly, though, I have never spent much time in the Old Testament.

Yes, there is much in the New Testament that can only be understood from the Old. But it is not necessary to know the entire Old Testament in order to understand God's plan for man.

One day, I was reading the Gospel of John. The next day, he saw Jesus coming toward him and said, "Behold, the Lamb of God, who takes away the sin of the world!" (John 1:29, ESV)

That was a eureka moment for me—one I could not ignore. Although I was familiar with the Day of Atonement, I wanted to go back and make sure I wasn't adding something that was not there. The rules for the ceremony of the Atonement are found in Leviticus 16. The pertinent verse is verse 21:

> "And Aaron shall lay both his hands on the
> head of the live goat, and confess over it
> all the iniquities of the people of Israel,
> and all their transgressions, all their sins.
> And he shall put them on the head of the
> goat and send it away into the wilderness
> by the hand of a man who is in
> readiness." (Leviticus 16:21, ESV)

All the sins of all the people were carried off into the wilderness. They didn't confess their sin. Aaron did. Aaron was the first high priest of the tabernacle. He is a type or shadow of Jesus.

John, in a moment of Holy Spirit revelation, saw the fulfillment of that Old Testament type in Jesus. What could his statement have meant to those who were standing around?

There was no introduction. There was no sermon with three points and a close—just a simple statement with reference to something they should understand.

And my world was changed forever.

Jesus takes away the sin of the world.

That is a plain statement of fact, but we have encumbered it with so much baggage that most people miss the depth of the truth presented here.

We have been taught, "Yes, but you have to accept it. It's a gift. Even though it is presented, if you don't accept it, you don't get it." That sounds logical enough from our perspective as finite human beings, but where is this concept taught in Scripture? Where's the verse that says, "You must choose Jesus"?

Most of the people who object to such thinking—such as Jesus taking all the sin of all the world—are usually those who insist on, "To the law and to the testimony: if they speak not according to this word, it is because there is no light in them." (Isaiah 8:20, KJV) They want at least one verse, preferably more, in order to prove a point.

Yet they cannot find a verse that plainly says one must accept the gift. They apply human logic to a few verses (which we will look at later) as their proof of the concept.

Because of this revelation in my spirit, I began to see the Bible in a whole new light. Passages that had remained dense for years came to life with a clarity I cannot "unsee."

I now see with different eyes. Much has changed for me in the last year or so. It is an ever-growing awareness of God's goodness toward us.

Come with me as I look through some of the Bible for these nuggets. I ask you, the reader, to make sure that I do not deviate from the truth of Isaiah 8:20, but that I stay within the confines of the plain written Word that God has given us.

May your eyes be opened to see the grandeur of God as the plan of salvation unfolds before you.

I pray:

> "that the God of our Lord Jesus Christ, the Father of glory, may give you the Spirit of wisdom and of revelation in the knowledge of him, having the eyes of your hearts enlightened, that you may know what is the hope to which he has called you, what are the riches of his glorious inheritance in the saints, and what is the immeasurable greatness of his power toward us who believe, according to the working of his great might..."
> (Ephesians. 1:17-19, ESV)

INTRODUCTION

WHAT THIS BOOK IS ABOUT

Many people are coming into this understanding from a strongly Bible-based background. Therefore, they need—and often require —biblical support for anything discussed. I hope this book will more than fulfill that legitimate desire.

Truth, in its first form, always elicits a certain amount of pushback. After all, the status quo is being challenged, and those with power within it will not readily relinquish their positions.

This also holds true for us on a personal level. Whenever we encounter something that challenges our beliefs about anything, our first response is almost always resistance. While the psychology behind this is deep, the essential truth is that we like what we know. That is our comfort zone. Anything that seems to contradict our beliefs has the potential to disrupt our comfort, and most of us would rather not deal with any amount of discomfort.

God's grace and His inclusion of all mankind in His purposes are at the forefront of revelation at this time. Multitudes are being influenced by this understanding. It does, however, challenge the long-held beliefs of many Christians, thereby causing a level of discomfort.

This, of course, is not the first time in the history of the Church that this understanding has come forth. As will be shown later, the idea of God's eternal love for all mankind was the main theme of the Church for the first five hundred years of its existence.

Is the idea that God's love extends to all creation for its eventual salvation a deception? Or is it the truth? How can we tell?

The only path I have known for the past fifty years is through the Bible. So that is where we will go in this book.

I want this to be a book about the subject of grace.

That is such an overwhelmingly large subject that I have been stymied from putting the first words to paper. It has taken me longer than usual to find a flow for the depth of what I want to present for your consideration.

I have tried to think in smaller terms—perhaps a smaller subject—but the more I study, the more I find that grace touches everything we think, say, and do in our lives. There is no aspect of our life with which grace is not concerned.

Is this a Bible study book? Yes.
Is this a book about grace? Yes.
Is this a book about salvation? Yes.
Is this a book about sin? Yes.
Is this a book about Jesus? Yes.
Is this a book about the Gospel? Yes.

Yes—it is all that and more. I want this to be a reference book on the concept of grace, to which you will return time and again.

WHAT YOU WILL FIND

You will find an abundance of Scripture references, most of which are commented on in light of the subject.

You will find definitions of words, because I have found over the past few years that people will challenge something said based on a different definition they already hold. My definition may not agree with yours, but at least you will know why I am writing in a certain way.

You will find specific treatment of certain words from the Bible that relate to the concept of grace.

You will find interpretations of specific passages from the three primary schools of thought concerning grace—Arminian, Calvinist, and Universalist. These are provided so that the reader can decide for themselves which view they find most compelling.

You will also find many objections people have to God's acceptance of all His creation.

The layout and format are simple.

You will find a chapter that explains an aspect of the understanding that God will eventually save everyone. This will be followed by an objection and my response to that objection. The specific objection may not necessarily be one commonly used against the passage discussed in the previous chapter, but it is a common objection to the principle itself.

In my previous book, I placed all the objections into one chapter, but that did not prove profitable for the reader—especially if the reader held an objection of their own.

This format will allow you to locate a particular objection of interest and see how it is addressed.

WHY I WANTED TO WRITE THIS BOOK

I have only recently embraced the idea that Jesus' work on the cross included all of humanity. Since the beginning of my walk with the Lord, I have come through each of the major schools of theology—Arminian, Calvinist, and now Universalism—in that order.

This, of course, does not mean that I am a Universalist. In fact, I have yet to find a clear definition of what a Universalist is or believes. Therefore, I do not want to be included within something that is not sure of itself.

There are a couple of terms with which I am currently comfortable, though I do not necessarily fully identify with them: "Hopeful Universalist" and "Inclusionist." These terms will be explained and developed later in the book.

As I have begun to share the understanding I am being given, there has been much pushback from those who object, but also much questioning from those who would like to know more. I hope this book will help each of them along the path of greater understanding.

The former group—those who object—seem mostly to have little understanding of the Scriptures concerning God's universal love and acceptance of all mankind. They often object simply because the idea contradicts what they believe the Bible says. I have found only a few who are ready to engage in meaningful conversation about these teachings. Perhaps this book will help open the door to further dialogue.

However, in all fairness, we have been taught to fear deception, and most objections arise from that place. Yet to think that any of us has arrived at all there is to know about God and His ways is deception itself—and the platform from which much false doctrine springs.

Therefore, while I truly believe what I have written here, I do not believe—by any stretch of the imagination—that I have arrived at all truth. Nor do I think that I have presented all the truth there is on this subject.

In fact, during my "final edit" of this book before sending it to the publisher, I was presented with two additional objections I had not previously considered. Following that, I encountered another passage that confirmed God's universal love for all. Each of these needed to be included, which required changes to the chapter order already established.

What you hold in your hands is the result of many hours spent reading Scripture, reading the thoughts of others, and posting snippets of what I believe on social media so that I could be confronted with objections.

I hope I have presented this material in a way that makes sense to you, whether you agree with me or not.

I humbly ask that if you find value in this book, you would share it with others. Buy them a copy, start a study group, or do whatever you can to help spread the word of God's unlimited mercy, grace, and love.

Thank you.

THREE THEOLOGICAL THOUGHTS

Salvation is a foundational concept in Christianity, central to the belief that humanity can be redeemed and reconciled with God. Within Christian theology, different perspectives exist on how salvation is understood and achieved.

There are three primary schools of thought about how humans are saved and come to know the eternal life found in Christ Jesus, our Lord. These are Calvinist, Arminian, and Universalist.

I offer these three perspectives as best I can and without commentary. You may find yourself in one of these perspectives, or a mixture of the perspectives, or you may be in a different place altogether. The following is a summary of each view.

> *NOTE: These thoughts are not my own, but are gathered from various sources to express—as much as possible—the uniqueness of each theological position.*

A CALVINIST PERSPECTIVE

One prominent perspective is Calvinism, a theological system developed by John Calvin during the Protestant Reformation.

Calvinism emphasizes the sovereignty of God in all aspects of salvation, highlighting divine initiative, predestination, and the concept of irresistible grace.

Calvinism is often summarized by the acronym **TULIP**, which represents its five key doctrines:

- **T**otal depravity
- **U**nconditional election
- **L**imited atonement
- **Ir**resistible grace
- **P**erseverance of the saints

Total Depravity: Calvinism starts with a view of humanity's fallen nature due to the sin of Adam and Eve. This doctrine asserts that every aspect of human nature has been affected by sin, rendering individuals incapable of choosing God on their own. Without God's intervention, humans are spiritually dead and incapable of initiating a relationship with God.

Unconditional Election: Central to Calvinism is the concept of predestination. Unconditional election teaches that God, in His sovereign will, chose certain individuals for salvation even before the foundation of the world. This election is not based on any foreseen merit or action of the individual, but is solely rooted in God's divine plan.

Limited Atonement: Also known as "particular redemption," this doctrine asserts that Christ's sacrificial death on the cross was intended specifically for the elect—those whom God had chosen for salvation.

Irresistible Grace: This doctrine teaches that God's grace, when extended to the elect, is irresistible and cannot be resisted or rejected by humans. When God chooses to draw an individual to Himself, that person will inevitably respond in faith and be saved.

Perseverance of the Saints: Often referred to as "once saved, always saved," this doctrine asserts that those whom God has elected and saved will never lose their salvation. God's work of salvation is secure and unalterable, ensuring the perseverance of believers until the end.

Embracing a Calvinist Perspective on Salvation

Humble Acceptance of Total Depravity: Embracing a Calvinist perspective begins with acknowledging the depth of human sinfulness and our inability to save ourselves. This recognition leads to humility, as individuals realize their desperate need for God's intervention.

Trusting in Unconditional Election: Trusting in God's sovereign election can bring comfort to believers, as they understand that their salvation rests not on their own efforts or merits but on God's unwavering purpose. This doctrine fosters gratitude and assurance in the believer's relationship with God.

Finding Assurance in Limited Atonement: Limited atonement can be difficult to understand, but it emphasizes the precision of God's redemptive plan. Rather than causing doubt, this doctrine reminds believers of the specificity and effectiveness of Christ's sacrifice for their salvation.

Surrendering to Irresistible Grace: Surrendering to God's irresistible grace involves recognizing that God's calling and drawing power are beyond human resistance. This surrender brings about a deep sense of awe and gratitude for God's initiation of the believer's salvation.

Resting in Perseverance of the Saints: The doctrine of perseverance of the saints provides assurance that God's work in salvation is unshakable. This assurance encourages believers to rest in God's faithfulness, even in the face of challenges and doubts.

Living Out a Calvinist Perspective

Pursuing Holiness: Embracing a Calvinist perspective on salvation calls believers to pursue holiness in their lives. This pursuit is not to earn salvation, but rather to reflect the transforming work of God's grace in their hearts and actions.

Sharing the Gospel Boldly: Calvinism underscores the sovereignty of God in salvation, but it also highlights the importance of sharing the Gospel with others. Believers are motivated to proclaim God's message of redemption, knowing that He will call and draw His chosen ones through their efforts.

Fostering Humility and Unity: Recognizing the sovereign grace of God promotes humility among believers. Understanding that salvation is a gift encourages unity within the body of Christ, as believers appreciate that they are all recipients of God's unmerited favor.

Praying for God's Will: Prayer becomes an avenue for believers to align their desires with God's sovereign will. Instead of seeking to change God's mind, prayers become a way to participate in His plans and purposes.

Cultivating Gratitude and Joy: Embracing a Calvinist perspective fosters gratitude for God's sovereignty, grace, and faithfulness in salvation. This gratitude leads to lasting joy, as believers find their security in God's unchanging character rather than their own fluctuating circumstances.

Calvinism offers a distinct perspective on salvation that underscores the sovereignty of God in every aspect of the believer's journey. Its doctrines encourage humility, gratitude, and assurance in the knowledge that God is the author and finisher of salvation. While embracing a Calvinist perspective may challenge some traditional notions of human agency, it ultimately directs attention to God's unfathomable love and grace. Whether one fully adopts this perspective or engages in thoughtful dialogue, the depth of Calvinist theology enriches the ongoing conversation about salvation within the diverse tapestry of Christian thought.

AN ARMINIAN PERSPECTIVE

Salvation lies at the heart of Christianity, offering the promise of reconciliation between humanity and God. Among the various theological perspectives on salvation, Arminianism presents a distinct viewpoint that emphasizes human free will, God's universal love, and the importance of personal response to the Gospel message.

Arminianism is named after Jacobus Arminius, a Dutch theologian who challenged certain aspects of Calvinism during the early seventeenth century. While diverse interpretations exist within Arminian theology, several core tenets characterize this perspective:

Human Free Will: Arminianism places a strong emphasis on human free will. It contends that God has endowed humanity with the ability to make genuine choices, including the choice to respond to the Gospel message in faith or reject it.

Conditional Election: Unlike the unconditional election of Calvinism, Arminianism proposes a view of election that is conditioned upon God's foreknowledge of human choices. God, in His omniscience, foresees who will respond to His grace and chooses them for salvation.

Universal Atonement: Arminianism affirms that Christ's sacrificial death on the cross was intended for all of humanity. Christ's atonement is seen as a provision that extends to every individual, inviting them to respond in faith and be reconciled to God.

Resistible Grace: Arminianism suggests that God's grace can be resisted or rejected by humans. While God's grace is essential for salvation, individuals have the freedom to accept or reject it, making their response a crucial factor in the process.

Conditional Security: Arminianism differs from Calvinism in its view of perseverance. It holds that while believers are initially saved through faith, they can choose to turn away from God and lose their salvation if they persistently reject His grace.

Embracing an Arminian Perspective on Salvation

Acknowledging the Gift of Free Will: Embracing an Arminian perspective begins with recognizing the gift of free will. God has granted humans the capacity to make meaningful choices, including the choice to accept or reject His offer of salvation.

Responding to God's Universal Love: Arminianism highlights God's universal love for humanity. Embracing this perspective involves understanding that God desires the salvation of all people and that His offer of grace is extended to everyone.

Engaging in Personal Faith: Arminianism emphasizes the significance of personal response to the Gospel message. Individuals are encouraged to actively engage with the message of salvation, exercising their free will by choosing to believe in Christ.

Cooperating with God's Grace: Embracing Arminianism involves cooperating with God's grace in the process of salvation. While God initiates the offer of salvation, individuals play an active role by responding to His call and working in conjunction with His grace.

Nurturing a Vibrant Relationship: An Arminian perspective encourages believers to cultivate a dynamic and authentic relationship with God. Personal growth, prayer, and obedience are seen as integral components of a faith journey.

Living Out an Arminian Perspective

Sharing the Gospel Freely: Arminianism emphasizes the universal nature of Christ's atonement. Believers are motivated to share the Gospel with others, knowing that God's offer of salvation is available to all.

Embracing Humility and Compassion: Recognizing the importance of human free will encourages humility and compassion toward those who have not yet responded to the Gospel. Believers are called to approach others with understanding and empathy.

Pursuing Discipleship: Arminianism encourages ongoing discipleship and spiritual growth. Believers are motivated to continue seeking God, studying His Word, and growing in their understanding of His will.

Seeking God's Guidance: Prayer becomes a means of seeking

God's guidance and wisdom in the choices individuals make. Arminian believers value seeking God's will in their decisions and relying on His guidance.

Finding Assurance in Personal Faith: While Arminianism does not guarantee unconditional eternal security, believers can find assurance in their ongoing faith and relationship with God. Trusting in God's faithfulness and grace provides a sense of security.

Arminianism offers a unique perspective on salvation that emphasizes human free will, God's universal love, and the importance of personal response to the Gospel. This theological framework encourages believers to actively engage with the message of salvation, responding to God's call with faith and cooperation. While embracing an Arminian perspective may diverge from other theological viewpoints, it underscores the idea that salvation is a dynamic process involving collaboration between God's grace and human response. Ultimately, whether one fully adopts this perspective or engages in thoughtful dialogue, the principles of Arminianism contribute to the rich tapestry of Christian thought surrounding salvation.

A UNIVERSALIST PERSPECTIVE

Universalism, as a theological perspective, asserts the ultimate reconciliation and salvation of all individuals, emphasizing the all-encompassing love and mercy of a benevolent Creator. According to universalism, the ultimate goal is for every soul to experience God's redemptive love, leading to unity, restoration, and transformation.

A Universalist perspective does not include various aspects or doctrines of how salvation occurs, but simply asserts that everyone will eventually come to salvation. In that place, the following shows how a believer responds to a life in Christ.

Recognize the Inclusivity of Divine Love

At the heart of universalism is the recognition that God's love is all-encompassing and transcends human boundaries. Embracing a universalist view of salvation begins with understanding that no one is excluded from the scope of God's love and mercy, regardless of beliefs, actions, or circumstances. This recognition forms the foundation for one's spiritual journey toward reconciliation and wholeness.

Cultivate Compassion and Understanding

A central aspect of universalist salvation is the cultivation of compassion and understanding for all individuals. This involves acknowledging the inherent worth of every person and seeking to understand their unique journeys. Practicing empathy and treating others with kindness aligns with the universalist belief in the ultimate redemption of all souls.

Embrace Personal Growth and Transformation

Universalist salvation emphasizes restoration and transformation for every individual. Embracing this perspective involves actively participating in personal growth and self-discovery. Engage in self-reflection, pursue self-improvement, and seek to align your life with the values of love, compassion, and unity.

Foster Hope and a Positive Outlook

Universalism encourages believers to foster hope in the ultimate reconciliation of all souls with God. Accepting universalism helps cultivate a positive outlook that sees the potential for goodness and growth in every individual.

Nurture a Relationship with the Divine

Universalist salvation invites believers to nurture a deep and meaningful relationship with the divine. Engage in spiritual

practices such as prayer, meditation, and contemplation to connect
with the transcendent. Seek moments of stillness and reflection to
align heart and mind with the belief in God's all-encompassing love.

Share the Message of Love and Inclusivity
Those embracing universalist salvation are encouraged to share the
message of love, inclusivity, and hope with others—communicating
that God's love extends to all, regardless of background or belief.

Practice Forgiveness and Reconciliation
Forgiveness is a vital aspect of universalist salvation. Practicing
forgiveness—toward others and oneself—is seen as a path toward
healing and reconciliation.

Advocate for Justice and Equality
Universalist salvation aligns with efforts to advocate for justice,
equality, and human dignity, promoting a world in which everyone's
inherent worth is recognized.

Find Comfort in Divine Love and Justice
Universalist salvation offers comfort in the belief that God's love
and justice ultimately lead to redemption. Trust in the divine
purpose that transcends human understanding, allowing this belief
to bring peace and assurance.

Conclusion

Universalist salvation presents a perspective of all-encompassing
love, reconciliation, and transformation. By recognizing the
inclusivity of divine love, cultivating compassion, embracing
personal growth, and nurturing a relationship with the divine,
individuals are encouraged toward unity and wholeness. Through
positive action, forgiveness, justice, and hope, universalist salvation
becomes a guiding force in shaping a more compassionate world.

Finally

Each of these positions informs various aspects of the remainder of this book. Objections come from one or another of the schools, as well as from the factual presentation of the chapters themselves.

Hopefully, when you reach the end of this book, you will have a firm foundation for your belief.

My goal, as always, is to "present each person perfect in Christ Jesus" (Colossians 1:28).

GENERAL OVERVIEW
DEFINITIONS

It's important that we're talking about the same things as you move through these pages. Too often, people argue over an issue while using two entirely different definitions. I don't want that to happen here.

You don't have to agree with my definitions, but you do need to know what I mean when I use them. If you're working with one definition and I'm working with another, we're not really communicating.

All — sometimes used as hyperbole, as in *"all Jerusalem,"* but more often meaning everyone, as in *"all those in Adam."*

Bible — the collection of sixty-six books beginning with Genesis and ending with Revelation, divided into the Old and New Testaments.

Heresy — a belief or opinion considered outside the accepted norms of traditional Christian doctrine.

Hyper Grace — a pejorative term applied to those who believe the grace of God knows no limits.

Inclusion — the belief that everyone who has ever been created is held within the love of God and His plan of redemption.

Orthodox — conforming to what is generally or traditionally accepted as right or true; established and approved.

Salvation — the condition of being completely and wholly right with God.

Scriptures — anything contained within the sixty-six books of the Bible. This does not include the Apocrypha, the Book of Enoch, or the Gospel of Thomas.

Sin — a disease within a person's being that causes them to manifest behaviors not in their best interest.

Sins — anything a person may do that goes against the love of God; also referred to as trespass or iniquity.

Universalism — the teaching that everyone who has ever been created will be saved.

Ultimate Reconciliation — the teaching that everyone who has ever been created will eventually be saved. This often includes the devil.

Brief History

One of the most comical—and at the same time sad—objections thrown at me has been, *"You're teaching something the Church has never heard before."*

It's unfortunate that anyone would make that kind of statement without doing even minimal research. If they had, they would have discovered that the concept of God extending salvation to all humanity was taught by notable thinkers in the early Church.

I'm older than the one who said that, but even I was taught this in the Catholic high school I attended. To be clear, it was presented as one of the early heresies the Church had to contend with, but there was still an awareness that the teaching of universal salvation existed centuries before the modern era.

Origen (185–253 AD) is most famous for having held this belief, though that is not what he is famous for. He is more widely known for his Neo-Platonic philosophies and his treatise *On First Principles*.

His association with the teaching of universal salvation is known because he was condemned as a heretic for holding this belief. However, it was not until 543 that Emperor Justinian I condemned him as a heretic and ordered all his writings to be burned.

Notice that it took almost three hundred years for this to happen.

There had been many challenges to Origen's teachings prior to this, but none had been taken seriously by those in theological leadership positions. Once the Church and the state were "married" under Justinian, all sorts of "problems" were dealt a death blow by those who wanted to control the populace.

I will explore the historical realities of these teachings in the next chapter, but this is sufficient to render the objection laughable. Origen had such a wide influence through his writings that much of the Church was shaped by his thinking.

Another theologian who was (and still is) highly revered in the Church was Gregory of Nyssa, also known as Gregory Nyssen, who was Bishop of Nyssa in Cappadocia from 372 to 376 and from 378 until his death in 395.

While not specifically known for his teachings concerning the universal restoration of all things, there are indications that he certainly believed such.

Again, this will be explored more fully in the next chapter.

Essentially, for the first five hundred years of the Church's existence, the belief in God's saving love for all mankind was an established orthodoxy.

Current Awakening

The doctrines of grace are currently (2023) experiencing a revival among believers of all stripes. Denominational people and pastors are hearing these things taught by teachers across the Body of Christ. People outside the realm of denominations are learning that God is not mad at them.

Obviously, this challenges the status quo of the churches as they exist today. The doctrines of fear and accountability are no longer finding many adherents. There are people who have not yet heard what God is doing in the realm of understanding His love and who are opting out of the system that has kept them in bondage for much of their Christian life.

What we are witnessing is a definite *"move of the Spirit"* around the world. Those who still need to see signs and wonders are questioning this movement because the only healing taking place is emotional and spiritual. No one is being "slain in the Spirit." No one is getting their legs lengthened. No big-name preacher is drawing crowds to himself. It is simply liberty being proclaimed to the captives through the all-encompassing love of the Father.

This is the first revival in centuries that truly exalts Jesus. All the others emphasized the sinfulness of man and his need for a remedy, which was to be found in Jesus.

This time, we are hearing all about Jesus—how He came to reveal the Father; how He is the exact image and representation of the Father; how He is the fulfillment of all things ever spoken by the prophets.

Jesus is at the forefront and center of this current awakening.

Yet, for some, all they hear is a single aspect of this glorious time, and they stop their ears because, to them, it is heresy.

How can an emphasis on the love of God become heresy?
Continue reading to discover the answer to this question.

1
A BRIEF HISTORY

Fact or Fiction

The teaching that God's eternal love is extended to all people at all times, resulting in the salvation of everyone, is a relatively new teaching of the modern era.

DISCLAIMER

Trying to discover the theology of the Church in the early days of its existence is not too difficult. It is a laborious exercise, to be sure, but not an impossible one. Much of the writings by the early church leaders are preserved and available to the modern reader.

Thanks to the multitude of scholars who have given themselves to a life of study, we now have great collections of letters, treatises, polemics, and sermons from those who have gone before us. And now, thanks to modern technology, a vast majority of these works are available to anyone who cares to examine them.

Scholars are able to distill their research and make it palatable and understandable for anyone. For instance, consider the massive (890 pages) volume *The Christian Doctrine of Apokatastasis* by Ilaria Ramelli. At the time of this writing, this volume sells for $345 on Amazon.[1]

Therefore, much of what I present in this section is not my own, but that of others who have paved the way for our understanding.

To the best of my ability, I will cite all resources—especially quotes —as a footnote at the bottom of the page. If it is discovered that I have plagiarized anything, I apologize in advance and ask for the grace and opportunity to make it right. I read extensively and sometimes fail to recall from whom I gleaned something.

I recognize and admit that I have had very few original thoughts in my life and that all my work is "built on the foundation of the apostles and prophets, Christ Jesus himself being the cornerstone" (Ephesians 2:20), and on many of the giants of the faith who have gone before me.

With that said, I present to you my humble offering on the early years of Christian doctrine as they apply to the topic at hand.

EARLY EXEGETES

The main thrust of this book is to present for your consideration the many places in the Bible that show us the inexhaustible, all-inclusive love of God for His creation. Therefore, the period of the New Testament Scriptures is purposefully not included here, as I will be delving quite deeply into these.

What happened after the apostle Paul left the scene? What was the Church teaching after John, the Beloved Disciple, left this plane?

There is, of course, no easy answer to this question. The Bible contains much more than simple explanations about our common salvation. So, there was a wide range of doctrines being taught—

---

1. *taken from the internet 5/5/23*

some good, some not so good. There were many of the Early Church Fathers who wrote quite extensively, arguing against what they considered the heretical teachings of their day.

Those so-called heresies ran the gamut of thoughts about Jesus, the Holy Spirit, the virgin Mary, how to interpret the Scriptures, and many other doctrines. My focus here, however, is specifically on what was being taught about salvation, judgment, and punishment.

A word that is often used in reference to a universal salvation is *apokatastasis* (ἀποκατάστασις). This Greek word is sometimes spelled in English with a 'c' instead of the 'k.' It is used only once in the Bible but is often used by the Patristic Fathers.

> It is found in Acts 3:21: "whom heaven must receive until the time for restoring all the things about which God spoke by the mouth of his holy prophets long ago."

However, a related word, usually translated as *restore*, is used eight times in the New Testament and 32 times in the Septuagint (LXX), the Greek translation of the Old Testament written 250 years before Christ.

The meaning of both words is "to put back into its original condition."

Peter used the healing of the beggar as a launching pad for an opportunity to preach to the crowd. The beggar was restored—put back in the condition designed for human beings—to that which God originally intended.

I find it interesting that Peter only made the claim about Jesus and the restoration of all things. He did not bother to tell us specifically about that to which he referred. He said that God had spoken of this restoration by the prophets of old.

Consequently, the verse from his sermon on Solomon's Portico has caused quite a bit of controversy over the centuries.

How do we determine what Peter meant? Was that another revelation that completely bypassed the brain of the thick-headed disciple, much like his revelation that Jesus was the Christ (Matthew 16:16)?

There are a multitude of variations and thoughts on his meaning provided by an array of theologians, beginning with those who came immediately after the apostles.

One of the most famous exegetes of the post-apostolic fathers is Origen, who was from the catechetical school in Alexandria. Because he was such a prolific writer, he is also the subject of much research and discussion concerning his views.

He wrote about all things spiritual that might be of concern to the Christian. He also wrote extensively, with great force of logic, against the heresies of his day.

More than a few researchers have delved into his thinking on *apokatastasis*, which he used as the basis for his exegetical works on numerous passages.

> "Following Clement, Origen appreciated the notion of *apokatastasis*, and he used it as an effective tool in his debate against the Gnostic dualistic worldview. This world is created in a perfect way by One Supreme God who loves every creation.
>
> Thus, despite the existence of sin, death, and evil in this world today, God will restore its original perfect state at the end of times. Therefore, according to Origen's interpretation of *apokatastasis*, it refutes completely the Gnostic notion of the idea of the exclusivity of salvation (i.e., only the elect ones will be saved).
>
> As a result of recognizing the importance and effectiveness of the notion of *apokatastasis*, Origen selected biblical texts to support it. 1 Cor. 15:24–28 is considered the basis of Origen's *apokatastasis*."[2]

---

2. Author's Note—*The above quote of three paragraphs was taken from the internet on 3/29/23. I have no idea who I took it from, as my computer went down in the process. It may have*

While Origen held to the doctrine of the salvation of all people, it was not the main thrust of his teaching or ministry. Fredrick W. Norris maintained, however, that Origen may not have strongly believed in universal reconciliation at all. In an article on *apokatastasis* in *The Westminster Handbook to Origen* (2004), he wrote, "As far as we can tell, therefore, Origen never decided to stress exclusive salvation or universal salvation, to the strict exclusion of either case."[3]

However, that is what he seems to be most noted for, which is probably due to his being branded a heretic three centuries after his death.

Why did it take so long for the Church to anathematize Origen and brand him as a heretic?

ORTHODOXY

We must go back to the early days of the Church after Jesus' ascension to heaven and consider the events from Acts 15. This chapter gives us the account of Paul and Barnabas going to Jerusalem to check in with those who had personally been with the Lord. They had a question about some teachings that were beginning to show up.

Some were claiming that in order for a Gentile to be a Christian, he must be circumcised, but Paul was adamantly opposed to this. Therefore, the first Jerusalem Council was convened to establish an orthodox belief. Peter helped in this council by recalling how God had used him at the home of Cornelius (Acts 10), and that no one was required at that time to be circumcised.

come from one of the many excellent articles found at: https://www.scribd.com/docs/Religion-Spirituality/Christianity
3. Taken from the internet 3/31/23— https://en.wikipedia.org/wiki/History_of_Christian_universalism#cite_note-25

This was the first official "Statement of Faith" or "These Things We Believe." These "statements of faith" have become the sine qua non of today's churches. While an individual church may not label you a heretic for not subscribing to their statement, it is almost guaranteed that you cannot be in fellowship with them if you do not agree with, accept, and abide by their statement.

This concept of orthodoxy did not become a major factor in the Church for a few hundred years. Heresies were not determined by councils, but by individual theologians who believed differently from the heretic. Orthodoxy, much like the law, became a way to determine who was acceptable and who was not.

We see this among the Jews who opposed Jesus during His ministry, especially with the healing of the man born blind (John 9). His parents refused to say how their son was healed for fear of being put out of the synagogue: "His parents said these things because they feared the Jews, for the Jews had already agreed that if anyone should confess Jesus to be Christ, he was to be put out of the synagogue" (John 9:22).

Even the authorities of that time feared the Jews and wanted to maintain their position. Orthodoxy was the driving force. "Nevertheless, many even of the authorities believed in him, but for fear of the Pharisees they did not confess it, so that they would not be put out of the synagogue" (John 12:42).

It was Origen's allegorical interpretation of Scripture that caused the most concern among the leaders of the Church after his death.

> "Argument over the orthodoxy of Origen's teachings spawned the First Origenist Crisis in the late fourth century, in which he was attacked by Epiphanius of Salamis and Jerome but defended by Tyrannius Rufinus and John of Jerusalem. In 543, Emperor Justinian I condemned him as a heretic and ordered all his writings to be burned."[4]

---

4.   *(Taken from the internet 3/31/23— https://en.wikipedia.org/wiki/Origen)*

"It is curious that, when Origen's theology was later condemned, it was not for his universalism, per se, but for his theory of repeating aeons. A little more than a hundred years after Origen's death, Gregory of Nyssa would also preach universalism, but without using repeating aeons. He instead proposed that universal salvation was a single eschatological event. It is interesting that Gregory's universalism was never condemned by a church council."[5]

Because he believed and taught the salvation of all people, and because this doctrine is so controversial due to Augustine of Hippo's influence, Origen is mainly remembered as holding the so-called heretical position of universalism. There are men of lesser renown who lived before and after Origen who also espoused the magnanimous love of God, but they are little known except among church historians.

What is known—not only by historians, but also by anyone faintly familiar with church history—is that controversy over doctrine never let up after that first Jerusalem Council.

There were constant arguments—mainly by way of written articles—against another's interpretation of Scripture as being heretical.

As the Church became more powerful and influenced the current government of the time, these treatises were written and presented to civil authorities in hopes of stopping any "new" teaching or doctrine. This often ended up with the one being attacked being labeled a heretic in order to preserve peace in the region.

Eventually, due to the growth and amalgamation of the Church with the government, the accepted orthodoxy became the rule of faith for all within the confines of that governing body.

This was true while the Catholics were in power and then continued when the Reformers gained power. Essentially, anyone who believed

---

5. (Taken from the internet 5/15/23 *http://www.pietisten.org/iii/2/ekman.html*)

differently from the accepted creed was a heretic, and heretics must be rooted out and destroyed.

The Reformation had almost as much persecution of heresy as the Inquisition of the Catholic Church in its time. What we fail to see behind the historical accounts is that "Might determined Right."

Therefore, to argue that this doctrine of restoration has never been accepted by the Church is specious at best.

Consider the following quote.

According to Dr. Edward Beecher's scholarly work, *History of Opinions on the Scriptural Doctrine of Retribution*, the following was the factual state of the early catechetical schools on this issue:

> "It was, in brief, this: There were at least six theological schools in the Church at large. Of these six schools, one, and only one, was decidedly and earnestly in favor of the doctrine of future eternal punishment. One was in favor of the annihilation of the wicked. Two were in favor of the doctrine of universal restoration on the principles of Origen, and two in favor of universal restoration on the principles of Theodore of Mopsuestia. It is also true that the prominent defenders of the doctrine of universal restoration were decided believers in the divinity of Christ, in the Trinity, in the incarnation and atonement, and in the great Christian doctrine of regeneration; and were, in piety, devotion, Christian activity, and missionary enterprise, as well as in learning and intellectual power and attainments, inferior to none in the best ages of the Church, and were greatly superior to those by whom, in after-ages, they were condemned and anathematized" (Beecher, 1878, chapter 22).[6]

The Great Schism of 1054 divided the Church into two separate major camps, one of which (Eastern) still holds to the teaching of Hell as a state of being rather than a place. The Eastern Church (by and large) believes there is a state beyond death where believers

---

6. https://salvationforall.org/7_History/2-catechetical_schools.html

continue to be perfected. This is similar to the Catholic concept of Purgatory, except the Catholics hold it as a place of punishment rather than a place of growth.

The history of "orthodoxy" is long, bitter, and lacking in any true authority. It is simply the result of the "majority opinion" of those accepting that which they have been told. Therefore, "the orthodox position" is not necessarily the best place upon which to stand.

It is the passing of time that establishes any orthodox position. For instance, the doctrine of Original Sin was never known until Augustine of Hippo (354–430 AD) introduced it into the Church. Today, it is almost commonly accepted as the teaching of the apostles, but none of those men ever said anything about it in their recorded writings.

However, the appeal to orthodoxy is still a common attempt to derail anything "new" from penetrating the mind of the average pew-sitter.

Fr. Lawrence Farley of the Orthodox Church in America has written:

> "I suggest that the recent interest in Universalism—the belief that everyone will eventually be saved—is the latest fad. Evidence of this may be found in the fact that the view is being promoted by a number of different people who have little contact with one another and with little else in common, such as by scholar David Bentley Hart (in his essay *God, Creation, and Evil*), and also by Rob Bell (in his best-seller *Love Wins*). Admittedly, the conviction that everyone will eventually be saved, including Satan and the demons, has been expressed from time to time throughout Christian history, but the majority of Christians have decided to pass on it. For people like the Orthodox who believe that God guides His Church and that, therefore, consensus matters, the solid fact of Christian consensus about the eternity of Hell is surely significant.

I suspect that one reason a belief in universalism is becoming popular is that our Western culture has lost its sense of sin."[7]

I would argue against his last statement about having lost the sense of sin. It was the emphasis on sin that has cost the Church its influence in the world. The emphasis on sin continued to instill a sense of fear, of which the world eventually grew quite tired—and reasonably so.

We are told why in John's first letter:

> "There is no fear in love, but perfect love
> casts out fear. For fear has to do with
> punishment, and whoever fears has not
> been perfected in love" (1 John 4:18).

A new understanding of the love of God is now being brought to the Church. Throughout history, whenever something "new" has been brought out, there has always been massive resistance.

Galileo (1564–1642) was ordered to turn himself in to the Holy Office to begin trial for holding the belief that the Earth revolves around the sun, which was deemed heretical by the Catholic Church because it taught the Earth as the center of the universe.

The Anabaptists, of whom the Amish, Hutterites, and Mennonites are, were denounced for their belief in the universal salvation of all. The Augsburg Lutheran Confession of 1530 denounces them in Article 17: "Our churches condemn the Anabaptists, who think that there will be an end to the punishments of the condemned and devils."

The Anabaptists were heavily persecuted for their belief in rebaptizing. They hold strongly to believer's baptism, rejecting any

---

7. (https://www.oca.org/reflections/fr.-lawrence-farley/will-everyone-eventually-be-saved
   taken from the internet 5/15/23)

form of infant baptism. This is how they came by their name, which means "rebaptizers." While this is still the main belief of these groups, not all Anabaptists today believe in the eventual restoration of all things.

All the so-called doctrinal heresies of the past have met with resistance, and so have the modern doctrinal heresies that go against established orthodoxy. This is nothing new, and according to history, nothing to fear. Truth will eventually win, if only for the individual believer (John 8:32).

The truth of salvation being brought to all humanity has its roots in the Bible, both in the Old and the New Testaments. It has been taught by different people throughout the Church age, of which we are now a part. It continues to be taught by many and is gaining popularity with the average person, not trained in theology, nor attached to the false belief that God's justice is explained by man's sense of justice.

Verdict: Fiction

This understanding has been with the Church since its inception.

2

OBJECTION— WHAT ABOUT...

Fact or Fiction

The Bible can be used to contradict itself

One of the most frequent objections used against any teaching on the universal love of God for all His creation comes in the form of *"What about…?"*

I often refer to these as "gotcha" verses. I will explain some of these verses in more detail later in the book.

Regardless of the verse or passage being presented, the objector will often respond with something like, "What about all the verses that mention hell?"

Sometimes (though rarely), the objector will list a specific verse that seems to disprove the point being made.

While I was traveling and teaching for five years, I stopped in at my original home church. I had attended the little Bible school the church sponsored, and I was eventually sent out into ministry. (That is a story all by itself, but for another time.)

I was just beginning to understand things about the grace of God—some of which went against what we had been taught in our evangelistic churches.

I was given the pulpit on a Sunday morning and began sharing from John's first letter and his Gospel.

Toward the end, I made a statement I have long regretted due to its foolishness at the time.

I said, "And if you are hearing eternal security, then you are hearing something."

I have since learned that there was no need for that remark. Just let the Holy Spirit do what He wills with each individual heart according to their level of understanding in the moment.

A woman came up to me afterward with tears in her eyes and asked if that meant her son was probably in heaven. Even though I didn't understand fully at the time, *"Yes"* was the only correct and comforting answer in that moment.

That evening, the associate pastor got up and very angrily went through many verses used to disprove the teaching of the security of the believer.

I gained a very valuable insight that night.

When we use the Bible to disprove something someone said *from the Bible*, the appearance is that the Bible contradicts itself.

Paul warned us about doing that in his second letter to Timothy:

> "Remind them of these things, and charge
>   them before God not to quarrel about
>   words, which does no good, but only ruins
>   the hearers" (2 Timothy 2:14).

The ruination of those who hear these arguments should be taken into consideration when we want to raise an objection to something someone has said or posted on social media.

Sadly, that is not the case with those who have appointed themselves the guardians of truth.

If that lady had been there that night to hear the rant, would she have been "ruined"?

When a verse of Scripture is used to disprove another verse of Scripture, the only logical conclusion for those not familiar with theology is that the Bible contradicts itself.

What should we do? How should this type of objection be handled?

If you are challenged with a *"What about...?"*, do not try to answer the objection. Instead, ask the objector to explain what they see as wrong with what you said *without using contrary Scripture*.

What they are essentially saying is:

MY VERSE TRUMPS YOUR VERSE.

In other words: 'Your verse can't mean what it plainly says, because my verse exists.'

WHY?

Why should that be?

Whenever someone challenges with "What about (Bible verse such and so)," they are essentially saying they have a verse that trumps the verse you are using. We call those "gotcha" verses.

This method of argument has been known as *proof-texting*.

Proof-texting is not a new thing. The Reformers used this method frequently in formulating their doctrines at the time.

In our own time, the rise in popularity of the Scofield Reference Bible has all but solidified this approach to learning what the Bible teaches. This may seem like the best approach to understanding the

Bible, but it often ignores the context and the author's original intent. (See Chapter Three on reading the Bible.)

Why should you go on the defensive?

If the one objecting has not yet said why they do not accept the verse you are using, then they are essentially saying the Bible contradicts itself.

In this sort of debate, it is important for the challenger to offer a differing viewpoint of the verse you are presenting from the verse itself before attempting to challenge it with another verse.

For instance, consider this verse:

> "Therefore, as one trespass led to
> condemnation for all men, so one act of
> righteousness leads to justification and life
> for all men" (Romans 5:18).

It would be necessary for the objector to show why the second "all men" in the verse is a different number than the first "all men." Then, you could go on to answer whatever objection they may have.

There is probably not a single concept of Scripture that cannot be proven "wrong" with a different verse. This is so easy to do that it has become the default mode—that is, proof-texting—for those who are on the lookout for something with which to disagree.

But Luke tells us there is a better way in Acts 17:11:

> "Now these Jews were more noble than those in
> Thessalonica; they received the word with
> all eagerness, examining the Scriptures
> daily to see if these things were so."

Notice that he says the Bereans searched the Scriptures to see if these things were so. They were not looking to prove Paul wrong simply because he was saying something they had never heard before.

They wanted to prove him *right*.

Whatever you focus on will become a reality for you.

When you are looking to disprove something, there is no shortage of research, ideas, and opinions available to help you—and you will see them almost immediately.

> **Consider this:** whenever a truth is heard for the first time, it will almost always create a negative reaction in the hearer.

Your comfort zone of "this is what I believe" is being challenged. Your intellectual security demands that you challenge this new thought, because if this new thing is true, then it would appear that you have been believing a lie.

No one desires to be caught believing a lie. Consequently, we will fight against the new thing to maintain our integrity.

Is your consistency of belief worth more than the truth?

Therefore, the first thing to do with any new truth from the Bible is to examine it by itself, without resorting to any other verse, passage, or concept.

What is the objector saying about *this* verse? Does it align with the way the verse is written? If so, then how do I handle any opposing concept?

If not, why not? If the person's interpretation is incorrect, why is that so? Explain it based on the verse of Scripture they are using—not with contrary verses.

Is this difficult?

Absolutely!!

It is not the way we have been trained to think.

You will find this process extremely difficult and challenging for those who object to what you are saying about the universal love and forgiveness of God for all humanity. Most will not be able to do it.

Therefore, a different path may be necessary—one that may actually be a bit more gentle.

Try to understand the paradigm they are coming from and bring that to light before attempting to answer the challenge. How are they viewing Scripture? What is their concept of God?

> Our understanding of particular verses comes from the filters through which we view Scripture. These filters are the result of the paradigm we use to understand things.

If your paradigm for understanding God is that of justice, then you will see everything in the light of *tit-for-tat, eye-for-eye*—people getting what they deserve.

If your paradigm for understanding God is love, you will see everything in that light. You may struggle with understanding some things in the light of love, but that is your paradigm, and it will serve you well.

A paradigm of *justice* cannot accept something that seems to contradict it and cannot be "set on the back burner" for more light and understanding. It must demand justice for all.

However, a paradigm of *love* will accept something that seems to contradict a verse, passage, or concept, and then let it "crockpot" for a while until the Holy Spirit gives understanding.

Therefore, when you are challenged with a "What about…?" your immediate response should be, "Okay. What about it?"

Do not be put in a defensive position of trying to explain yourself before you know where they are coming from. Put the ball back in their court.

They need to explain themselves more fully, or else you will only be trying to answer an assumption on your part.

Usually, this will reveal whether the person is curious about what you are saying or simply being antagonistic. If the latter, there is no need to engage further, as there is no desire on their part to learn.

A person who is curious may not come around to agree with what you are saying, but they will not be antagonistic. If it is a truth for them to understand, that will happen in God's timing.

If they are antagonistic, Solomon also warns us not to engage:

> "Do you see a man who is wise in his own
>   eyes? There is more hope for a fool than
>   for him" (Proverbs 26:12).

For me, as soon as someone raises their voice in argument, I am done. Debate and dialogue are no longer possible—only a heated argument with two people trying to prove they are right.

Debate and dialogue are vehicles for learning.
Argumentation is a vehicle going nowhere.

Do not despise sincere debate, for it will help sharpen your understanding. "Iron sharpens iron, and one man sharpens another" (Proverbs 27:17).

THE GOOD STUDENT

Regardless of where you are in your understanding of the Bible, you should be on the pathway of becoming a good student of its contents. That is what Jesus meant when He told the apostles to "make disciples of all nations" (Matthew 28:19).

The phrase *"make disciples"* translates from a single Greek word meaning *"to enroll as a learner."* We are all learners in the things of God, regardless of which school of theology we may subscribe to.

With the abundance of Bible helps available today, there is no reason anyone should not be a good student of the Bible.

Using a topical approach, you can find a multitude of verses that speak to whatever concept you may be researching. *Nave's Topical Bible* is the most well-known work for this. You can also use the *Thompson Chain Reference Bible*, which is what the Lord used for me during my initial training.

Strong's Exhaustive Concordance to the Bible is a monumental work and has been the study resource for several generations of students. In its print form, it is very difficult to master, but with modern technology, it is now available to anyone. Learning to use it correctly, however, requires a course of study in itself.

Modern Bible apps give us even better tools to understand what the Bible teaches. It is now possible to find every place a single Greek or Hebrew word is used and how it is translated into English.

With these tools at hand, you will want to find every verse or passage that deals with the topic you are studying—including those that seem to contradict your premise.

You will be forced to consider how the verses that seem to contradict your premise fit into the overall picture.

That is where true study and enlightenment begin.

With "gotcha verses" already in hand before you are challenged, you will be more prepared to "give a reason" to all who ask (1 Peter 3:15).

Finally, do not despise those who challenge your position, whether they are curious or antagonistic. They come your way to help you, not hinder you. They give you an opportunity to articulate more clearly what you believe.

> "Let all things be done in love, for the
>   purpose of strengthening one another" (1
>   Corinthians 14:26).

Verdict: Fact

The Bible can be used to contradict itself—but that does not mean it does so in reality.

3
READING THE BIBLE

Fact or Fiction

The Bible should be read the same as any other book

According to the Guinness Book of World Records, "The best-selling book of all time is the Christian Bible. In the 21st century, Bibles are printed at a rate of around 80 million per year."[1]

This does not account for excerpts from the Bible such as The Gospel of John, or copies of just the New Testament, or children's Bibles.

Even though many homes have a copy of the Bible somewhere gathering dust, it is still the most-read book of all time.

How should we read this Book of Books? Is there a way to read the Bible that helps with our understanding of its contents?

In my almost 60 years of teaching the Bible, I have heard many say

---

1. (https://www.guinnessworldrecords.com/world-records/best-selling-book-of-non-fiction
Taken from the internet 5/27/23)

we should read the Bible through each year. Many tell new believers to begin with Genesis and read the Bible straight through.

I am so grateful the Lord did not allow me to hear such nonsense when I began my journey with Him. I would have ended up like most others who follow that pattern when first beginning—quitting by the time I got to Numbers.

The writer of Hebrews opens his letter with a very interesting observation:

> Long ago, at many times and in many ways,
>> God spoke to our fathers by the
>> prophets, but in these last days he has
>> spoken to us by his Son, whom he
>> appointed the heir of all things, through
>> whom also he created the world.
>> (Hebrews 1:1-2)

Do you see that little word "but"? "But" is a conjunction that contradicts everything that came before it. While the words of the prophets may have a little value for us, our current thinking—and the bending of our ear—should be toward the Lord Jesus.

Since the life and ministry of Jesus are the focal point of our Christian faith, why not begin by reading the Gospels?

Learn about Jesus—what He taught, how He thought, what He did. Learn about His death, burial, and resurrection. Learn about His miracles. Learn about His parables.

That is enough to keep the new believer occupied for more than a year.

Then read the epistles of Paul. He gives us an understanding of how the things Jesus did and taught apply to us today.

What you won't learn from either of these teachers is how to view the Bible.

Who wrote the Bible?
To whom was the Bible written?
For whom is the Bible written?
Is every word in the Bible for us today?
Are there some things that have little to no meaning for us?

How you view the Bible and its contents will determine much of what you believe. Your view will influence which teachers you listen to and which themes or doctrines you espouse—and which ones you reject.

The Bible is an anthology—a collection of various stories written by many different men and women over the course of a few centuries. It also contains poetry and history, neither of which is read in the same manner as a historical account or a theological dissertation, such as Romans or Hebrews.

How are we to view those stories? Are they simply opinions expressed by people influenced by the society of their time? Are they true records of events as they happened? Do these stories portray for us the mind and heart of God toward His creation?

It is this last question that causes us the most difficulty, and the answer varies among believers.

Evangelical believers have been taught that the Bible is the inspired Word of God, without error, and sufficient for our understanding of God and His ways with us and for us.

Is that the truth?
Is that how God wants us to approach this collection of books that only a few men and women have decided are the only books God approves?

Most teaching on this subject uses 2 Timothy 3:16 as its anchor point.

All Scripture is breathed out by God and profitable for teaching, for reproof, for correction, and for training in righteousness.

This verse has been taught as, "The Bible was inspired by God and is profitable…"

The problem lies with the word "Scripture."

The first problem with this line of thinking is that Paul wrote this to Timothy long before there was anything in writing that would be called the New Testament. Yet this verse is used in a kind of circular reasoning to prove the inspiration of the entire Bible.

Sadly, the logical fallacy of this approach is lost on many believers.

PLEASE UNDERSTAND

Simply because I do not accept this fallacy does not mean that I do not believe the Bible. If you read this book to the end, you will discover that I have a great love for the Book of Books and that I continually reference it.

The second problem associated with using this verse is, again, the word "Scripture." We read that word with only a single definition in mind—"Bible."

The word translated as *Scripture* is the Greek word *graphe*, which simply means "writing," or "the thing written."

What Paul wrote to Timothy is that **all writing** that is inspired by God is profitable for his use as an elder in the church (SEE VERSE 15).

We all benefit from the writings of others who have endeavored to share with us the things God has inspired in them. Therefore, the first thing we should understand is that God has inspired more than just the various people who have written parts of the Bible.

All God-inspired writing is profitable for our walk with the Lord.

This should bring up the obvious question: "How do we know what is inspired and what is not?"

Good question.

Easy answer—we don't.

And that is also true for the Bible.

We have only assumed the Bible is inspired because that is what we have been told by those who want to protect us from ourselves.

Please don't misunderstand—this should not be a cause for alarm.

Due to being told what and how to believe by others who seem to have more intelligence than the rest of us, we have failed to believe Jesus and His words.

> "When the Spirit of truth comes, He will guide you into all the truth…" (John 16:13)

This is what we should have been taught—not dependence on someone else to tell us what and how to believe.

Doesn't this allow for a multitude of interpretations? **ABSOLUTELY.** But how is that any different from what we already have with more than forty thousand denominations worldwide?

If the Bible is to be our guide, then we must learn to believe what is revealed to us individually, rather than looking to others to form our beliefs.

This is not to say that we do not benefit from teachers, for we do. I am attempting to teach through the writing of this book. If I have been inspired by God, and you come to this book under the inspiration of the Holy Spirit, then the Lord may quicken something to you as you read, making it alive and real for your benefit.

I believe that great damage has been done to the Church by submitting all our authority to others rather than to the Lord.

So…let's consider some more of the things we have been told about the inspiration of the Bible.

THE CANON OF SCRIPTURE

- Who determined what should be a part of our Bible?
- Why did they choose some books and not others?
- What was their criteria for making those decisions?

These are not questions without answers, because the history of our Bible is well known. The Bible, with its sixty-six books as we have it today, has gone through numerous iterations, with various individuals proposing an acceptable canon at different times in history.

> *NOTE—for an online presentation of the history of the development of the canon of our Bible, go to Wikipedia at:* http://bit.ly/4jla8Re

I have no desire to present you with the history—or even a synopsis of the history—but rather to show you that what we have today has not always been the case. Even now, there is still debate over which writings are authentic and which are not.

For our part, as believers living in the twenty-first century, we can accept what has been commonly referred to as the Bible. However, among the various denominations, this is not consistent, since some accept the Apocrypha as an inspired part of the Bible.

INSPIRATION

The concept of inspiration is the biggest problem and the cause of much division within the Church. In order to stem the tide of division caused by this, the *Chicago Statement on Biblical Inerrancy* (1978) makes the following assertions:

Article V

We affirm that God's revelation within the Holy Scriptures was progressive.

Article VI

We affirm that the whole of Scripture and all its parts, down to the very words of the original, were given by divine inspiration.

> There are many more articles of affirmation and denial contained within the statement, which can be found at: https://www.thegospelcoalition.org/themelios/article/the-chicago-statement-on-biblical-inerrancy/

In and of itself, the affirmations can be accepted as they stand. However, the interpretation and application of these kinds of statements have greatly influenced our thinking in a detrimental fashion.

Article VI states that the inspiration was "down to the very words of the original…" While it is not possible to mount a logical argument against this claim, it is still problematic for our understanding.

There are no original manuscripts still in existence. All we have are copies of copies, which were all handwritten.

Some have tried to tell us that God inspired the copyists so as to prevent mistakes, but this is patently false. We have too many variations within the copies available to us.

The average reader, being told that the Bible is the inspired Word of God, only knows to apply everything in the Bible to themselves. Books on how to study the Bible tell us to look for the application of each verse to our own lives. This may be a noble exercise, but it is not the way we should read the Bible.

Our understanding is limited by at least four things:

- Education
- Culture
- Vocabulary
- Language

The first three of these filters are part of the following true story from my experience.

There was a young girl who came to our church. She was raised on the streets and had little education. Her love for what the Lord had done in her life was undeniable and quite contagious.

One Sunday morning, she stood to give testimony to something the Lord had shown her.

She said, "I was reading in the Bible and came to the Our Father. I read the words 'Our Father who art in Heaven,' and I realized that God loves art."

We may snicker at her naïveté, but it serves to illustrate my point.

Was she wrong in her conclusion?
Of course not.
God has inspired most of the art we have today.

Was she wrong in her interpretation of the verse?
Yes.
Her interpretation could not be used to develop a doctrine with which to teach others.

God used that moment in her life to inspire her. We can applaud that, just as we did that morning.

I know that we expect our scholars and those who guide us to have a better understanding than she did, but we are still left with a multitude of influencers who do not necessarily have much breadth in the four areas of our limitations.

For instance, you may have been told that the word *agape* in Greek was a word invented by Paul to describe the unconditional love of God. I heard this often during my formative years as a teacher. I have heard it recently from some very popular—and good—teachers, but they are wrong. They were simply repeating something they heard without checking it out for themselves.

The Septuagint (LXX), which is the OT translated into Greek 250 years before Christ, used the word to describe the love Jacob had for Rachel in Genesis 29:18.

Is *agape* used to describe the unconditional love of God? Yes—but let's not give it more due than it deserves.

Jesus told us to love our enemies with this *agape* love: "But I say to you, Love your enemies and pray for those who persecute you" (Matthew 5:44).

If *agape* love is strictly unconditional and universal, then we may need to rethink how we treat our enemies.

I know that what you have read so far may be a tough nut to crack —a hard pill to swallow.

Whom do we trust? Again, the only correct answer is "the Holy Spirit." He will guide us.

And that guidance into understanding may change over time— much like an aircraft or a ship at sea must alter its course occasionally in order to maintain proper direction toward its destination.

This is what Article V of the Chicago Statement brings out so beautifully: "God's revelation within the Holy Scriptures was progressive."

This progressive revelation should inform our understanding and interpretation of the Bible.

However, since the concept of "every word is inspired" has taken root, most believers are still stuck, trying to duct-tape their theology together so it all fits into one consistent stream.

Even though many discover this to be an exercise in futility, they have not managed to find a satisfactory alternative.

Grasping the truth of progressive revelation will solve many problems of interpretation and consistency.

If someone has walked in the things of God for more than five years and nothing has changed in their understanding, then they have grown in grace very little.

A progressive understanding would bring them into new heights of joy and depths of understanding, with each contributing to a greater love for God and humanity.

PROGRESSIVE REVELATION OF GOD

In the same way that a child grows in its understanding of its parents, so we should be growing in our understanding of God.

This truth is clearly revealed in the Bible as we consider the concepts men and women held of God from the beginning of their writings about Him until the last of their writings. The book of Revelation is excluded here because of its intensely symbolic nature; therefore, it is not a good presentation of God's nature.

The early history of humanity, as recorded in the Bible, reveals a people who were afraid of a "Great Spirit" they could not comprehend. Their world was filled with terror and terrible things happening all around them—things they attributed to God.

Then Jesus appears and tells us that He has come to reveal the Father. Jesus said to Philip:

> "Have I been with you so long, and you still
> do not know me, Philip? Whoever has
> seen me has seen the Father. How can you
> say, 'Show us the Father'?" (John 14:9)

How violent is Jesus?
Was the justice He called for equal to an eye for an eye?
Did He require that we memorize and follow an impossible list of rules in order to please God?
Did He not break down all the rules and regulations of the Old

Testament into two simple thoughts—love God and love your neighbor?

Is this not the conclusion reached by John when he wrote, "God is love"? (1 John 4:8)

Can we not see the progressive revelation of the Father as we read the Bible story as it unfolds, rather than picking out our favorite verses to prove a particular point?

Therefore, any teaching that does not originate from an understanding of Jesus will likely lead us down the wrong path.

In other words, the idea that God could wipe out entire nations must be understood in the light of Jesus, who said, "Love your enemies." This is not the place to try to reconcile those two concepts, but it *should* give us pause as we consider how we read and understand the Bible.

Perhaps seeing Scripture through the lens of progressive revelation is too much for some people, which is a distinct possibility given the limitations mentioned earlier. However, with consistent Bible reading, an open mind, and a heart tuned toward the Father's heart, some things will eventually become self-evident.

When we first encounter them, we may struggle to understand. Over time, however, our minds may be opened to a different possibility.

For example, most of us have believed that it was God who established the sacrificial system for the Hebrews when they came out of Egypt. That is how we have been taught, and that is how we have believed.

A closer look at the Bible may reveal a different conclusion.

Jesus consistently referred to "the Law of Moses," never calling it God's law: "Has not Moses given you the law? Yet none of you keeps the law. Why do you seek to kill me?" (John 7:19)

The idea that sacrifice was required by God is challenged by David, Solomon, Samuel, Jeremiah, Hosea, Micah—and Jesus Himself when He says: "Go and learn what this means: 'I desire mercy, and not sacrifice.'" (Matthew 9:13)

David

Psalm 40:6 (ESV)
"In sacrifice and offering you have not delighted,
but you have given me an open ear.
Burnt offering and sin offering you have not required."

Psalm 51:16 (ESV):
"For you will not delight in sacrifice, or I would give it;
you will not be pleased with a burnt offering."

Psalm 51:17 (ESV):
"The sacrifices of God are a broken spirit;
a broken and contrite heart, O God, you will not despise."

Samuel

1 Samuel 15:22 (ESV)
"Has the LORD as great delight in burnt offerings and sacrifices,
as in obeying the voice of the LORD?
Behold, to obey is better than sacrifice,
and to listen than the fat of rams."

Solomon

Proverbs 21:3 (ESV)
"To do righteousness and justice
is more acceptable to the LORD than sacrifice."

Hosea

Hosea 6:6 (ESV)
"For I desire steadfast love and not sacrifice,
the knowledge of God rather than burnt offerings."

Micah

Micah 6:6–8
"With what shall I come before the LORD,
and bow myself before God on high?
Shall I come before him with burnt offerings,
with calves a year old?
Will the LORD be pleased with thousands of rams,
with ten thousands of rivers of oil?
Shall I give my firstborn for my transgression,
the fruit of my body for the sin of my soul?"
He has told you, O man, what is good;
and what does the LORD require of you
but to do justice, and to love kindness,
and to walk humbly with your God?

Jeremiah goes even further, stating that God never required sacrifices. Or, more accurately, *the way we read the Bible records God as saying this*: "For in the day that I brought them out of the land of Egypt, I did not speak to your fathers or command them concerning burnt offerings and sacrifices." (Jeremiah 7:22)

If this is accepted as truth as revealed in Scripture, then it necessarily changes the way we read the Old Testament. We are forced to confront a possibility we may never have considered—that the Bible was written by men using the mind of man, attempting to convey their understanding of the supernatural according to their level of awareness at the time.

THE COVENANTS

Another factor that affects our understanding of the Bible is how we view the covenants.

Some focus on the many covenants found in Scripture, assigning varying levels of importance to each. These approaches are usually found in relatively small groups who believe they possess a clearer understanding of God than the rest of humanity.

Most of us, however, recognize two primary covenants: the Old Testament (OT) and the New Testament (NT).

In every Bible, just before the Gospel of Matthew, there is a page titled *The New Testament*. This division has shaped how we read and understand Scripture.

Yet within that division lies a problem we have largely overlooked— and as a result, we have misunderstood both the nature of the Bible and its importance for us.

Week after week, we sit under ministries that unintentionally reinforce this misunderstanding. Many teachers and preachers begin most of their sermons in the Old Testament. They draw lessons from the text and apply them to our lives. This is not inherently wrong.

Paul tells us:

> "For whatever was written in former days was
> written for our instruction, that through
> endurance and through the
> encouragement of the Scriptures we
> might have hope." (Romans 15:4)

However, a steady diet of the Old Testament trains the average believer to look there for their understanding of God and His ways —and *that* is where the problem lies.

Too often, these teachings revolve around "what God requires," which is not an accurate representation of the gospel.

Others claim that "the Old Testament informs our understanding of the New Testament." This is partially true. But again, as a steady diet, it becomes misleading.

The Old Testament has been superseded by the New Testament, and this must be firmly rooted in our understanding if we are to truly know God and His ways.

> "In speaking of a new covenant, he makes
> the first one obsolete. And what is
> becoming obsolete and growing old is
> ready to vanish away." (Hebrews 8:13)

The Old Testament is obsolete—not useful as a governing framework for our relationship with God. It does not present a full or accurate picture of Him.

How is a covenant—or a will—established? It only comes into effect after the death of the one who made it.

> "For where a will is involved, the death of the
> one who made it must be established."
> (Hebrews 9:16)

The New Covenant came into being through the death of Jesus.

Pause for a moment.

If Jesus' death was necessary to establish the New Covenant, how can the Gospels be part of the New Testament? The Gospels record His birth, life, ministry, death, and resurrection—yet they are included under the heading *New Testament*.

Something doesn't quite add up, and this further challenges how we interpret and understand the Bible.

If we begin to see the Gospels as a **transitional period** between covenants, many of Jesus' teachings suddenly make much more sense.

Bible publishers are unlikely to change a structure that has been in place for over a century. But *we* can think differently.

Rather than two sections, we may need to consider a third—call it whatever you wish—that represents the transition from the old covenant to the new.

Conclusion

These observations may cause a brief hiccup in the way you've traditionally viewed the Bible. Don't let that diminish your love for the Book of Books.

As these ideas settle into your thinking, you may find yourself seeing not only the Bible differently, but also the magnificence of the Creator with fresh eyes.

Verdict: Fiction

The Bible contains multiple genres and styles of literature that cannot all be read in the same way.

For an excellent discussion of these principles, see Unhook the Book by Don Keathley.

4
OBJECTION—
UNIVERSALISM
IS HERESY

Fact or Fiction

Believing a heretical doctrine has the potential of destroying the soul and should therefore be feared and avoided.

HERESY

One of the common objections against any thought of the universal salvation of all people is that it is heresy. Using the word "heresy," or calling something heretical, or labeling someone a heretic seems to put a certain fear in people so that they want to avoid that which has been so labeled.

The word "heresy" is laden with all sorts of connotations which affect the uninformed believer. The term has often been used by someone in authority to cause others to disassociate from the "heretic."

When pressed for a reason, though, the only thing that is usually said is, "It's heresy." No explanation as to the dangers of heresy or why something is heresy. The term is used by those "in authority" to keep those who are subject to them from learning something outside their stated orthodoxy.

This is what has happened to the teaching of God's universal grace, love, and forgiveness being extended to all humanity. It has been labeled as heresy. Consequently, many refuse to consider any teaching on the subject regardless of who the teacher might be.

What is heresy?
How dangerous is heresy to my salvation?
Who determines what is heresy?
How is orthodoxy established?

From the early days of the Church until now, heresy has always been a concern. We find the concern about heretical teachings within the writings of Paul the apostle, which will be considered later in this chapter.

Irenaeus (130–202 AD) was a student of Polycarp, who was a student of John the apostle. Irenaeus is famous for his book *Against Heresies*, in which he primarily targets Gnostics and their "secret wisdom." He also held that the surest way to avoid heresy and to follow orthodox teaching can be found within the Church of Rome.

Many others of the Patristic Era also put pen to paper, denouncing certain heresies and those who promoted them. Origen, one of the early Church Fathers who taught this doctrine, was labeled a heretic at the Second Council of Constantinople in 553. However, it should be noted that Origen had died 300 years earlier, in 253. He was never labeled as a heretic during his lifetime.

Therefore, in reality, the concept of universal salvation was a teaching of the early Church for 500 years. (Refer to chapter one for a more in-depth treatment of this.)

The Protestant Reformation saw a resurgence of polemics against heresies held by different individuals. The Reformation itself was labeled heresy by the Catholic Church. Within the ranks of the Reformers, different ones were called heretics by others.

A September 2022 issue of *Christianity Today* had an article on the "Top 5 Heresies Among Evangelicals Today."

There are massive volumes written outlining the major heresies that have confronted both Jewish and Christian understanding of God. It would appear, therefore, that heresy should be a major concern for the believer.

Definitions

Finding an exact or consistent definition of the word "heresy" is an exercise in futility, probably due to the nature of its use, which I will explore later. Therefore, for our purposes here, I have chosen to use a few from resources respected by the majority.

The Oxford Dictionary: belief or opinion contrary to orthodox religious (especially Christian) doctrine.

Merriam-Webster

a. adherence to a religious opinion contrary to church dogma
b. denial of a revealed truth by a baptized member of the Roman Catholic Church
c. an opinion or doctrine contrary to church dogma
a. dissent or deviation from a dominant theory, opinion, or practice
b. an opinion, doctrine, or practice contrary to the truth or to generally accepted beliefs or standards

We can see from Webster that the word is used in more than just a religious or theological sense.

Strong's Definition: αἵρεσις *haíresis*, hah'-ee-res-is; properly, a choice, i.e., (specially) a party or (abstractly) disunion.

Biblical Usage

The Greek word for heresy or sect is used nine times in the New Testament, six of which occur in the Acts of the Apostles and none in the Gospels. Isn't it interesting that Jesus never referred to heresy or called anyone a heretic?

The King James Version uses the word "sect" to translate the Greek word five times, referring to the Sadducees, the Pharisees, the Nazarenes, and the Christians.

The word "sect" is defined by Oxford Languages as—a group of people with somewhat different religious beliefs (typically regarded as heretical) from those of a larger group to which they belong.

This definition would have Christianity as the larger group and all the various expressions of the faith as a sect. This is not an incorrect view.

The Sadducees and Pharisees were sects of the larger group known as Jews. The Nazarenes and Christians were also referred to as sects by the Jewish leaders, but in a more derogatory tone. (SEE ACTS OF THE APOSTLES 24:5, 14)

Therefore, we are to understand that a sect is heretical by definition. The Bible translators, by and large, use the word "sect" to translate "heresy" throughout the Book of Acts.

In modern usage, we have become more comfortable with the word "denomination" to replace "sect." Every single denomination fits the definition of the word "sect" in that they are groups that have separated themselves from a larger group.

Therefore, by extension, every single denomination is heretical in nature. And if they are heretical, then they believe a heresy.

Hopefully, you are beginning to see just how foolish it is to fear the idea of heresy when it is not explained.

If a teaching is labeled as a heresy, then it is necessary to know what makes that teaching heretical. How does it deviate from the accepted norm? How does it deviate from orthodoxy?

Paul's Use of Heresy

We find the word for heresy only twice in Paul's writings.

> "For there must be factions among you in order that those who are genuine among you may be recognized." (1 Corinthians 11:19)

> "Idolatry, sorcery, enmity, strife, jealousy, fits of anger, rivalries, dissensions, divisions," (Galatians 5:20)

In the section from Galatians, the word is translated as *divisions* and is listed among the flesh rather than the fruit of the Spirit.

Notice that the word is within a list of things which contribute to divisions within the church—strife, jealousy, fits of anger, rivalries, dissensions, divisions, envy. Each of these results from a self-centered approach to life. It would be a major stretch to take the word *heresies* (KJV translation) and make it about doctrinal issues in this passage.

However, in his letter to the Corinthian church, it can be implied that doctrinal issues are being considered. The word for heresy is translated as *factions* in the English Standard Version and as *heresies* in the King James Version. Most of the other modern translations use *factions*, while a few use *divisions*.

Using the King James Version for our understanding of this verse leads us to believe that our church leaders are to recognize and point out any heretical teachings. This is what lends itself to the idea of doctrinal issues.

However, in the context of the issues Paul is addressing, we are once again left in an awkward position to make this about false doctrine. This verse is within the section on the church's practice of taking the Lord's Supper. We know from the beginning of the letter that Paul was addressing the various causes of division within the local church. In fact, the previous verse (verse 18) uses the word *schisms*, which in our language means divisions.

The ONLY place in the New Testament where the word for heresy refers to doctrine is found in Peter's second letter.

Damnable Heresy

The King James Version uses the word *damnable* in association with the word *heresies* as found in 2 Peter 2:1. The English Standard Version uses the word *destructive*.

> "But false prophets also arose among the people, just as there will be false teachers among you, who will secretly bring in destructive heresies, even denying the Master who bought them, bringing upon themselves swift destruction." (2 Peter 2:1)

Damnable seems to carry more weight in our thinking than destructive. The former is usually associated with some concept of hell, so the thinking is that heresy will damn the soul to hell.

All of our more modern translations, including the New King James Version, use the word destructive.

The Greek word used in this verse has a simple meaning—"loss or ruin"—yet one that is not limited in scope. It is usually associated with material objects and only by metonymy (that is, substitution) associated with hell when applied to persons.

Peter describes what he believes to be a damnable heresy as "denying the Lord who bought them." With this definition, it is easy to see why people believe that heresy will send one to hell. For most believers, denying the Lord means not accepting His offer of salvation.

> *NOTE: "Not accepting God's offer of salvation" is a theological fallacy which is dealt with in Chapter Six.*

Therefore, we are left to consider what happens to someone who denies the Lord. How are they "destroyed?" The common thought is that they are lost forever and sentenced to eternal conscious torment in the fires of hell.

Does that fit in with the rest of Scripture on this subject? Are there other places where this is the obvious meaning of "destruction?"

No.

Peter is the only one who uses the concept of heretical teaching to cause destruction for the person. That destruction must be viewed in the light of the rest of Scripture and the uses of the word for destruction.

At that point, we have a couple of options since there is no clear treatment of the destruction associated with the denial of the Lord within the Bible.

Destruction of the life lived on this plane of existence.
We see this regularly, with the terrible results of a life lived outside the knowledge and awareness of God's grace.

Destruction of some kind after this life.
This is a distinct possibility and should not be dismissed lightly. However, with what we know about eternal, we should not be led to believe that there is absolutely no hope for one in this position.

ORTHODOXY

If heresy is a deviation from orthodox beliefs, it is necessary that we understand the meaning of orthodoxy. In trying to do so, we are left with the same questions that apply to heresy.

What is orthodoxy?
How necessary is orthodoxy to my salvation?
Who determines orthodox belief?
How is orthodoxy established?

Definitions

Using definitions for words helps us to "stay on the same page" in our thinking. Without an agreed-upon definition, we are subject to arguing for or against something that exists only in our own minds and not necessarily with others.

According to Oxford Languages, our common use of the word "orthodoxy" means authorized or generally accepted theory, doctrine, or practice.

Obviously, this definition leaves too much "wiggle room" for a consistent conversation. "Generally accepted" by whom?

A stricter definition based on the meanings of the two Greek words that form this compound doesn't offer much help either. The word *orthodoxy* comes from the Greek roots *orthos*, meaning "right, true, or straight," and *doxa*, meaning "opinion." So orthodoxy describes the one true opinion.

We are still left with the question of who determines the "one true opinion."

Neither "orthodox" nor its cognates appear in the Bible, but the last part of the compound word—*dox*—does, which comes from the Greek word *doxa*. *Doxa* is used 168 times in the New Testament and is translated *glory* 145 times in the King James Version.

Going into the linguistic derivation that led from "opinion" to "glory" is too much for this chapter, but the "Outline of Biblical Usage" in the Blue Letter Bible app, and in Thayer's Greek Lexicon, show that the major meaning is that of "opinion." This is due to its use in the secular writings of ancient Greeks.

In a nutshell, then, "orthodoxy" is simply the opinion, theory, or doctrine determined by a group. To be orthodox, one must subscribe to the group's beliefs. As soon as one goes beyond the accepted truths of the group, then that one is no longer orthodox and has become a heretic.

Are you beginning to see just how foolish it is to fear the idea of heresy when it is not explained? If it simply goes against your group's standards, does that in and of itself make it wrong or dangerous?

When that group claims to have a handle on the truth, then YES, that makes it dangerous.

Does the "heresy" of universal salvation deny the Lord? No, it magnifies the Lord and what He did through the cross. This beautiful truth will be expounded and enlarged upon as you go through this book.

For our purposes here, though, we can see that when the true meaning of HERESY and ORTHODOXY is understood, people will see that the "heresy" of universal inclusion of all in God's salvation carries the same weight as a Baptist calling a Methodist a heretic.

Verdict: Fiction

Most heretical doctrines are simply ideas not accepted by a particular group, not necessarily ideas that can lead a person away from the Lord or into hell.

5
THE KEY

Fact or Fiction

The Old Testament reveals the concept of the universal salvation of all people.

During a casual reading of the Gospel of John, I was hit with a MAJOR insight. How many times had I read this passage and never seen its full intent? I was mesmerized and stopped reading in order to contemplate the significance of what the Holy Spirit had just revealed to me.

> *The next day, he saw Jesus coming toward him and said, "Behold, the Lamb of God, who takes away the sin of the world!"* (John 1:29)

Since a crowd had gathered with John on the Jordan, it is logical to assume this statement was spoken loudly enough for the crowd to hear. It was not something John muttered under his breath.

What did this mix of educated and uneducated Jews hear? What was the Baptist saying? The Lamb of God who takes away the sin of the world? What could he possibly be referring to?

These people did not have the later teachings of Jesus nor the letters of Paul with which to compare that statement.

It was a simple yet profound declaration:

This man walking among you takes away the sin of the world.

Do you think they may have included themselves in that statement? I certainly do. I don't think they transferred the thought to "those people out there." They also had no basis for assuming that any action was required on their part.

The conversation between Jesus and Nicodemus recorded in John 3 had not yet taken place, had not been written down, and had not yet been misinterpreted.

These folks were left with only their understanding as it related to their annual feast on the Day of Atonement.

"The lamb of God" had meaning for them. A lamb was sent off into the wilderness each year bearing the sins of all the people of Israel on its back. The high priest would then tell them they were forgiven and they could start fresh with their attempts to be righteous.

Therefore, this was obviously a strange statement by the Baptist. This was no ordinary lamb of the sheep family. This was a man.

Obviously, I was not in that group at that time, but the Holy Spirit made it so real to me that I may as well have been there.

JESUS—THE LAMB OF GOD

This was a declaration that should have surprised every person listening at that moment. Regardless of their education, every one of them knew the significance of the lamb of God. It was a part of their annual celebrations.

I was immediately taken back to Leviticus and the instructions for the Day of Atonement.

> And Aaron shall lay both his hands on the
>   head of the live goat, and confess over it
>   all the iniquities of the people of Israel,
>   and all their transgressions, all their sins.
>   And he shall put them on the head of the
>   goat and send it away into the wilderness
>   by the hand of a man who is in readiness.
>   The goat shall bear all their iniquities on
>   itself to a remote area, and he shall let the
>   goat go free in the wilderness. (Leviticus
>   16:21-22)

On the Day of Atonement, no one except the high priest made any confession of sin. No Jew had to lay his hand on the head of the goat as a *point of contact.* In fact, many of the Israelites were probably not present for this ceremony during the time of Jesus.

ALL the sins, iniquities, and transgressions of ALL the people were confessed and placed on the goat, which was then sent into the wilderness bearing their sin.

And ALL of the people of Israel were forgiven.

They didn't do anything. They didn't make any confession or express any repentance. They did not have to "accept" anything from the priest or anyone else.

The Baptist declares that this "Lamb of God" is not for Israel only or exclusively, but for the WHOLE WORLD!

This "Lamb of God" is the walking, talking, living, breathing fulfillment of the type and shadow of the Old Testament ceremony performed every year. He removes the sin of the whole world without so much as a "by your leave."

What the Day of Atonement did for all of Israel, the "Lamb of God"—Jesus—did for the whole world.

However, now that Jesus has a multitude of people who are able to interpret Him and His mission, there is now the thought that people must "accept Jesus" in order for their sin to be forgiven.

Do we really believe that the Baptist only had a partial revelation, and that the world needed the New Testament to be completed before we could accurately understand the meaning of salvation?

If we can take this passage at face value without any additions to it, then we might be able to understand those other verses in a different light.

Maybe "accepting Jesus," though not a biblical term or concept, means recognizing what has been accomplished for us.

That recognition will certainly change our perspective on life and the work of the cross.

If John the Baptist was the only person under the Old Covenant to utter such a concept, then we might have an argument against a face-value interpretation.

However, John was not alone in this understanding.

OTHER OLD TESTAMENT WRITERS

This group of verses contains the search phrase "all nations."

Psalm 67:2: ...*that your way may be known on earth, your saving power among all nations.*

The psalmist (a choirmaster) desires that the saving power of the Lord may be known and seen among ALL nations. The knowledge spoken of in this verse is more than just something "I recall having been told." It is the full recognition by all people of the truth being spoken.

Jeremiah 3:17: *At that time Jerusalem shall be called the throne of the LORD, and all nations shall gather to it, to the presence of the LORD in Jerusalem, and they shall no more stubbornly follow their own evil heart.*

Though figurative language is being used here, there is the thought that ALL NATIONS will be gathered into the presence of the Lord. Their rebellious heart is also dealt with, so it is not a case of "My way or the highway" on the Lord's part. No. The heart of everyone is changed to love the Lord.

Psalm 22:27: *All the ends of the earth shall remember and turn to the LORD, and all the families of the nations shall worship before you.*

What is it that the "ends of the earth" are to remember? It would appear that it has something to do with their having at one time been aware of their relationship to the Lord. When they "remember," they "return."

Psalm 45:17: *I will cause your name to be remembered in all generations; therefore, nations will praise you forever and ever.*

The same Hebrew word for "remember" is used in this verse as in the previous verse. And when they "remember," they will praise the Lord.

Psalm 86:9: *All the nations you have made shall come and worship before you, O Lord, and shall glorify your name.*

Many try to say that this only means "some people from every nation" will come and worship. Many of those people claim to interpret the Bible literally. However, a literal interpretation of this verse (and many just like it) requires that we understand it to mean "all nations."

Some people also claim that this is sort of like being made to "cry uncle" as someone forces you to the ground. But how is that "worship?" How is that giving glory to His name?

Do we truly believe that God is so desperate for acknowledgment that He will force His way onto others?

Isaiah 2:2: *It shall come to pass in the latter days that the mountain of the house of the LORD shall be established as the highest of the mountains, and shall be lifted up above the hills; and all the nations shall flow to it.*

ALL NATIONS shall flow to the mountain of the house of the Lord for the purpose of worship. Still the same idea of "all nations."

This next section contains the search phrase "every knee shall bow."

Isaiah 45:22-23: *Turn to me and be saved, all the ends of the earth! For I am God, and there is no other. By myself I have sworn; from my mouth has gone out in righteousness a word that shall not return: 'To me every knee shall bow, every tongue shall swear allegiance.'*

God has declared that EVERY knee will bow and EVERY tongue will swear allegiance. If that is "forced" in any manner, how is that a good thing? How is God honored in that? The Lord will then be just another bully on the stage of the human drama.

Psalm 65:2: *O you who hear prayer, to you shall all flesh come.*

Was this just wishful thinking on the part of the psalmist? Is it not possible that he had insight into the heart of God? It certainly appears that this is a definitive statement about the future.

Isaiah 11:9: *They shall not hurt or destroy in all my holy mountain; for the earth shall be full of the knowledge of the LORD as the waters cover the sea.*

The earth shall be full of the knowledge of the Lord, which will cause the cessation of those things people do when they do not know the Lord. We can see here a prophetic pronouncement for the future.

The whole earth will be full of the knowledge of the Lord.

Some will try to convince us that this means the wicked have been removed. If that is true, then why does the prophet make the first part of the statement about not hurting or destroying? Would it not have been better to proclaim that all wicked people are removed?

But that is not the case. The second clause begins with the word "for," meaning "because."

The knowledge of the Lord rules supreme over all the earth, including those who formerly were opposed to the Lord.

Psalm 66:4: *All the earth worships you and sings praises to you; they sing praises to your name.*

Obviously, the psalmist was not speaking of a present reality for his time. He was seeing something beyond the natural order. However, there is no getting around the fact that the concept of a salvation for everyone is foreseen in this verse.

Ezekiel 16:55: *As for your sisters, Sodom and her daughters shall return to their former state, and Samaria and her daughters shall return to their former state, and you and your daughters shall return to your former state.*

Does this not remind you of what Peter said in his first sermon on Pentecost? He declared that Jesus would be restoring ALL things to their former condition. (SEE ACTS 3:21) There was a time when Sodom, Samaria, and all those like them (their daughters) were righteous before the Lord.

Psalm 68:18: *You ascended on high, leading a host of captives in your train and receiving gifts among men, even among the rebellious, that the LORD God may dwell there.*

The Lord dwells among the rebellious? The Lord receives gifts from the rebellious? Did the psalmist know what he was talking about, or is our theology somewhat messed up? Surely, the Lord only dwells among the righteous (like us), right?

Could it be that maybe God is of a bigger heart than we have imagined?

Of greater love than we can conceive?

Psalm 145:9-10: *The LORD is good to all, and his mercy is over all that he has made. All your works shall give thanks to you, O LORD, and all your saints shall bless you!*

A person must do some amazing exegesis to show that this verse does not mean what it says. God is good to ALL, and ALL His works—the good and the rebellious—shall give thanks.

Isaiah 25:6-7: *On this mountain, the LORD of hosts will make for all peoples a feast of rich food, a feast of well-aged wine, of rich food full of marrow, of aged wine well refined. And he will swallow up on this mountain the covering that is cast over all peoples, the veil that is spread over all nations.*

The covering or veil that keeps people from seeing the love and mercy of God will be taken away by the Lord.

There are just way too many verses that hint at this future restoration of God's goodness being the reality of life for all people.

How is it possible that so many people are able to ignore this glorious truth?

There is one last clue from the OT that I would like to consider, which gives us a shadow of good things to come. (Hebrews 10:1)

YEAR OF JUBILEE

The year of Jubilee happened once every 50 years in the year following the 7th sabbath rest of the land (SEE LEVITICUS 25). This means that an entire generation could live and die without ever experiencing the Jubilee. Maybe they never even heard of such a thing.

There is no record of it having ever been observed, but the rules governing this feast are quite interesting. These rules may also be the reason the feast was never celebrated.

The rules and requirements for this feast are found in Leviticus 25:8-55. Details of many possible situations are given, but the essential thing to know is that everything was to be restored to its original condition.

Jubilee was the year when EVERYTHING returned to its original state for the Jews.

- Land was returned, whether it had been bought, rented, or otherwise occupied.
- Debts were forgiven whether paid off or not.
- Slaves and indentured servants were released from their bondage.

In other words, the Year of Jubilee celebrated the restoration of all things.

It was a time of great joy and celebration throughout the land—except for those whose wealth depended on lands, debts, and slaves. Because these are usually the types who are "in charge" and rule things, it is possible they are the reason there is no record of Jubilee ever having been celebrated.

Jubilee was a time of restoration—a restitution of all things (Acts 3:21). The feasts of the Lord instituted under the Old Covenant were types and shadows for something in the future. We see this in the major feasts with which most of us are familiar:

- Passover/Atonement = Jesus
- Feast of Weeks = Pentecost
- Tabernacles = (still under discussion by many)
- Jubilee = Restoration of all things.

There is a message being proclaimed around the world in this hour about this jubilee—this "acceptable year of the Lord" (Luke 4:19).

There are many who have never heard of such a thing. Some of these stand in awe at the possibilities, while others deny that such a thing ever entered the mind of God. However, for those with eyes to see, there is a celebration of freedom being experienced by those who were once bound by those in power.

No more will the people of God fail to keep the Year of Jubilee!

The *antetype* is fulfilled today and will last for the rest of time, as people will refuse the bondage of being used for another's gain in the religious world.

This newfound freedom has caused us to join the ranks of those who are eagerly expecting the full revelation of the sons of God so that all creation may be set free from the bondage of corruption into the glorious liberty experienced now by only a few (Romans

8:19-23). But those few are increasing into a critical mass from which there is no turning back.

Church history reveals that there has been a gradual restoration of the former truths once delivered to the saints (Jude 1:3), and the message today is the beginning of the fulfillment of which Peter spoke (Acts 3:21)—THE FINAL RESTORATION OF ALL THINGS.

Verdict: Fact

The Old Testament is replete with plain statements, types and shadows, and hopeful prayers for the salvation of ALL people.

6
OBJECTION— DESTROYS EVANGELISM

Fact or Fiction

There is no need for evangelism if ALL are saved.

This is a very common objection, heard often by those who begin to proclaim the truth of God's love and grace. Their friends and/or family will look at it without much study or knowledge and conclude that evangelism is unnecessary if all are saved. This is based entirely on their own reasoning, with absolutely no biblical support for their objection.

More times than not, I will ask a question when such an objection is presented—"When was the last time **you** shared the Gospel with someone?" I have yet to encounter anyone who will admit to having shared the Gospel recently, within the past month.

"So, then…why are you saying that what I believe—universalism— destroys evangelism? What has destroyed evangelism in your life?"

The point in this objection is a specious argument at best. It looks good on the surface, but it fails to address any sort of reality.

There is an underlying thought that there is no need to share the Gospel at all if everyone is going to be saved in the end. Of course, this kind of thinking comes from those who believe that it is necessary to believe the Gospel and accept Jesus in order to escape the punishment of Hell.

That is why people use the question, "If you die today, do you know where you will spend eternity?" However, to use this as a way to "preach the gospel" or "get people saved" is to completely miss the point of why Jesus came to earth. It completely misses the reality of the good news.

Jesus never used this question as a means of evangelism, nor did any of His apostles, including Paul. The Gospel is not about a futuristic, far-off afterlife, but about the reality of **now**. His mission was to bring people healing, deliverance, and restoration right here and now on this earth.

The Gospel has never been about escaping the fires of an eternal hell—three concepts which will be dealt with in later chapters.

The word "gospel" means "good news." Etymologically, it comes from an Old English compound of *god*, meaning good, and *spel*, meaning news, tidings, or discourse.[1]

Our modern presentation of the gospel, however, is lopsided by its bad news: "You are a sinner who has offended a holy God, and you must repent of your sin and believe the good news."

There is no bad news in the good news.

Jesus brought the good news of His ministry as recorded in Luke:

> "The Spirit of the Lord is upon me, because
> he has anointed me to proclaim good
> news to the poor. He has sent me to
> proclaim liberty to the captives and
> recovery of sight to the blind, to set at

---

1. *(Dictionary of Word Origins by John Ayto, Arcade Publishing, 1990, page 260)*

liberty those who are oppressed." (Luke
4:18)

Notice that He said He was to "proclaim good news." There is
nothing about any process for accepting the good news. Nothing
about repentance from sin, praying any kind of prayer, or joining
any group. Simply proclaiming the good news, which by itself would
accomplish the desired end of bringing salvation.

The phrase "proclaim good news" translates the single Greek word
euangelizō, from which we get our English word evangelize.

Think about the simplicity of what Jesus said and compare it to the
convoluted approach we now have to sharing the Gospel with pre-
believers.

In every "How to Witness" class or seminar I have ever attended,
the process of "sharing" was essentially the same and followed the
old, worn-out, man-made Romans Road.

1. Everyone has sinned.
2. You are a sinner.
3. Sin brings the death of hell.
4. God has provided a way out of that through Jesus.
5. All you have to do is believe this and say so in a prayer.
6. Now you are saved and on your way to heaven.

This program was developed from man's logic and a few verses of
the Bible taken completely out of context, and it has been used for
decades to increase the number of people occupying seats in a
church hall.

Were they "saved" through this program? That is not for me to say. I
know that the Lord is quite able to use whatever means He desires
to find those who are still wandering around on the outside,
looking in.

That program, though, is not the gospel nor the evangelistic model
which Paul gave us in his second letter to the Corinthians.

> "All this is from God, who through Christ
> reconciled us to himself and gave us the
> ministry of reconciliation; that is, in
> Christ God was reconciling the world to
> himself, not counting their trespasses
> against them, and entrusting to us the
> message of reconciliation." (2 Corinthians
> 5:18–19)

Paul says that we are given the ministry of reconciliation. We are to be the messengers who bring the good news to those who need to be reconciled. He then tells us **exactly** what that good news is—in Christ God was reconciling the world to himself, not counting their trespasses against them…

If God is not counting anyone's trespasses against them, why do we think it is necessary to tell them they are sinners?

NO!

The truth is, "God is not mad at you!" That is good news for those who have lived their lives in fear that "God's gonna get you for that!"

For those who claim that the message of "God loves you and is not mad at you" destroys evangelism, it is necessary that they first get clear on the contents of the Gospel.

Secondly, we should understand what evangelism means.

Those who object, saying that belief in the restoration of all things destroys evangelism, have a very weak understanding of either concept—evangelism or the universal love of God.

As already noted, evangelism comes from the Greek word meaning to speak good news.

We have "Christianized" this word to make it mean much more than was intended by Jesus or Paul.

When someone is "brought in" via the Romans Road, they are then told what they must or should do now that they are saved.

1. Find a good church
2. Read your Bible
3. Tell others about what has happened to you.

Number three is a real bugaboo. Maybe nothing has "happened" to the person. What can they tell about what "happened?"

According to those who preach this ethic, sharing what has happened will strengthen your faith.

In addition to the psychological reasons, they are told to tell others, they are told they are also fulfilling the Great Commission by this action.

THE GREAT COMMISSION

The so-called "Great Commission" is the basis for getting everyone to share the gospel, to tell others about Jesus. It is often treated as equal to the two Great Commandments that Jesus gave us.

Is it?

The statement of Jesus to His disciples to go into all the world and make disciples of all nations has been grossly misunderstood.

> "Go therefore and make disciples of all
>   nations, baptizing them in the name of
>   the Father and of the Son and of the
>   Holy Spirit, teaching them to observe all
>   that I have commanded you. And behold,
>   I am with you always, to the end of the
>   age." (Matthew 28:19–20)

What Jesus told the apostles has been taken and applied to every single believer. Everyone is to make disciples. Yet, in its application by those who tell us to fulfill this mission, they do not allow believers to exercise every part of it.

Unless you are "in the ministry," you are not allowed to baptize, and unless you are recognized by your church, you are not allowed to teach.

Why is this broken down and compartmentalized in such a manner?

The full mission is either for all believers or it is not.

However, most new believers will not pick up on this discrepancy and will believe what they are told. For many, like me, that belief makes us feel guilty when we do not share the good news.

The simple truth is—**not everyone is called to share the good news.**

Sure. When a golden "can't-miss opportunity" is presented, we should indeed share the truth of Jesus. But that doesn't happen to everyone every day.

Each of us has a gift from the Lord by the Holy Spirit for the purpose of building up the Church. (Ephesians 4:12) (A good study would be to learn about all twenty-one gifts mentioned in the New Testament.)

> I have a ten-page report which goes into much detail on the Great Commission, which you can find here, or by going to—https:// practicalbibleteaching.com/re-thinking-series/the-great-commission/

Those of us to whom the Lord has revealed these truths of His eternal love for all His creation are very much on the forefront of evangelism. We see how people have been held captive by a legalistic bondage which Paul declared to be "another gospel." (Galatians 1:7–8)

We take these truths with us into churches that have invited us, and we sometimes are asked to leave afterward. Still, we preach. We take these truths online and share them via Facebook, blogs, YouTube, and other social media platforms.

The result?

We are seeing the masses respond to the good news that has been withheld from them by those who would keep them in bondage to a false gospel.

We see the absolute and overwhelming need for evangelism due to the misrepresentation of Jesus and the Gospel.

We desperately want to see people set free from the bondage religion has placed them in and brought into the glorious liberty awaiting those who are longing to be free from corruption. (Romans 8:21)

Salvation is much more than being rescued from a pathway to hell so as to go to heaven when you die. Salvation is about the freedom awaiting those who learn the truth in this life and are thus able to live accordingly. (John 8:32)

HOW TO BE SAVED

In Chapter Four, I dealt with the concept of heresy and tried to show that the term "heresy" is not as dangerous as we have been led to believe. Basically, any difference of understanding with another person puts both parties within the realm of heresy.

I also stated that "accepting Jesus as your personal Savior" is a theological fallacy. And within the context of understanding God's universal love, grace, and mercy to all people of all time, we must deal with the question, "What about those who don't accept Jesus?"

It is not possible to dismiss this question with a simple statement, because the concept of accepting Jesus has been taught for decades and is now in our collective psyche as the "truth."

But it is not the truth, and there is more than one aspect of fallacy in this concept.

If it is up to humans to accept God's offer of salvation in order to be saved, then that places the human race as superior to God's power. Those who claim that God *had* to give us free will so that we could "choose" to love Him fail to see how this makes us more powerful than God.

We are left with a caricature of God wringing His hands, "hoping" that humans will "accept" what He has "tried" to do for them. However, once we are able to see the teachings of the Bible which proclaim that He is the "Savior of all," then we can see that our will is subservient to His will.

Because we have been stuck for so long with "you must accept Jesus," we are not able to see any other way that salvation is effected.

"Accepting Jesus" is supposedly supported by two separate verses.

> "But to all who did receive Him, who
> believed in His name, He gave the right
> to become children of God," (John 1:12)

> "Because if you confess with your mouth that
> Jesus is Lord and believe in your heart
> that God raised Him from the dead, you
> will be saved." (Romans 10:9)

John's statement in his Gospel is used to prove that we must "accept" Him. You must put out your hand to "receive" a gift.

Seems logical.
But it's false.

First, this verse was written concerning those people in Israel during the time of Jesus' ministry. Those who "welcomed" Him and His teaching ministry are those who "received" Him.

By extension, we can apply this verse to our modern day as welcoming Jesus, or believing Him and His teachings. However, this is not the same as "accepting" Him according to the modern vernacular.

"Accepting" is now used in a logical progression of thought presented as "The Roman Road to Salvation," mentioned earlier. It is presented in a salesmanship framework, in which the one who needs to be saved is presented with a set of conditions and must respond.

- You're a sinner.
- You will go to hell if you don't repent.
- You don't want to go to hell, do you?
- God has provided the escape if you will accept Jesus as your personal Savior.

This "process" is cobbled together from a selection of verses—none of which present this so-called reality.

You will not find any sermon or explanation in the New Testament that comes anywhere near this concept. If the apostles and the other writers of the New Testament never saw this "truth," why do we think it should be presented as such?

No one warned of hell.
No one warned of the dangers of failing to repent and its consequences.
No one said anyone must "accept Jesus" to be saved.

Does this not mean that maybe we have "added" to the Scriptures? (Revelation 22:18)

Second, in the verse in Romans, the word "if" is emphasized as a condition one may refuse, but that is not necessarily its meaning.

The word is most often used to indicate a future condition of which the speaker may not be aware of the outcome.

Paul was not saying, "If you refuse, then you are going to hell." That is nowhere in Paul's writings, nor is it anywhere else in Scripture.

All that is necessary to understand what I am saying is to read the context of this verse. Do not try to make the verse stand alone on its own merit without the context.

Paul said, "The word of faith is already within you." And when you finally understand, you will confess with your mouth that Jesus is Lord.

The passage is not teaching a doctrine of free will, but a doctrine of what *must happen*—much like "you must breathe." Breathing is not something you can accept or reject like obeying the speed limit.

Yes—in one sense of the word, we must "accept" Jesus in order to be saved, but it is not something we can simply reject due to our supposed superior free will. It is something that must—and will—happen to everyone, according to God's perfect plan and timing.

> "And I, when I am lifted up from the earth,
>   will draw all people to myself." (John
>   12:32)

Just because we are not able to see the process or the event with everyone does not mean that Jesus did not speak the truth. He *will* draw everyone to Himself. Of that you can be sure.

In the great passage of Romans chapter ten, Paul concludes with the concept of evangelism. Prior to this, he has gone to great lengths to show that everyone—both Jew and Gentile—will be saved.

He says that evangelism is the necessary key for everyone to hear.

> "How then will they call on Him in whom
> they have not believed? And how are they
> to believe in Him of whom they have
> never heard? And how are they to hear
> without someone preaching?" (Romans
> 10:14)

Far from destroying evangelism, the good news of the salvation of all is the *catalyst* for true evangelism.

Verdict: Fiction

Evangelism is the necessary tool the Lord has chosen to set people free from bondage.

7
ETERNITY EXAMINED

Fact or Fiction

Eternity Means Time Without End

The teaching of universal salvation is based on Scripture and on the proper understanding of words and their meanings. Much harm has been done to the thinking of the Body of Christ through using only the English rendering and understanding of terms.

As stated in Chapter Three, our understanding of anything is limited by at least four things:

- Education
- Culture
- Vocabulary
- Language

Our religious training affects our cultural understanding. A cursory examination shows that Catholics believe differently about salvation than their Baptist friends, who believe differently than their Methodist friends, who believe differently than their Pentecostal friends, *ad infinitum, ad nauseam*.

Limited to only our cultural understanding of things, we will hardly ever move beyond whatever our culture has (in)formed us.

As we begin to add to the mix an education, an understanding of our language, and an increasing vocabulary, we may begin to see more than what has been presented to us within the narrow confines of our culture.

For instance, I was raised in the South as a Catholic. After I left home and began to explore different parts of our country, I learned that my experience was vastly different from that of most Northern Catholics. This opened my eyes to the importance and influence of culture on one's worldview.

While my vocabulary is not nearly as extensive as many of my peers, I have learned to use a thesaurus, which enables me to choose and use a variety of words with similar meanings. Hopefully, this helps my writing not be so boring due to redundant expressions.

I have a fair command of the English language and am able to express myself in a way that is understood. I have also taken on the task of learning the Greek language of the New Testament, but I am in no way a scholar. However, I know enough to be able to use resources not readily available to the average Bible student.

With the limitations given above, it should be apparent why we have so many different denominations and theologies. Many preachers are in the pulpits teaching the Bible from within the very narrow limitations mentioned. They have not availed themselves of the blessings God has provided by allowing us to stand on the shoulders of some very great men and women of God who have joined the Church Triumphant.

Consequently, their hearers remain as limited in their understanding as the teacher from whom they are learning. Without an awareness of the expanse of language, we would be hard-pressed to understand the line from Led Zeppelin's *Stairway to Heaven*—"'Cause you know sometimes words have two meanings...'"

It is this multiple-meaning aspect that has caused much of our problem with biblical interpretation, and without knowledge of it, we would be limited even more than we are now.

Let us examine one of those words that goes into the informed understanding of most universalists—*eternity*.

Our basic English definition of the word is *'infinite' or 'unending' time.*[1]

The main theological understanding of the word is *endless life after death.*

Neither of these definitions coincides with the definition of the Greek word, which is translated as "eternity" or its cognates.

The word *eternal* appears 68 times in the King James Version of the New Testament and only 4 times in the Old Testament.

The word *forever* never appears in the King James Version of the New Testament, but it is used 49 times in the English Standard Version. The word does not appear in the Old Testament of the King James Version, but it is used 331 times in the English Standard Version Old Testament.

Everlasting is used twenty-six times in the King James Version New Testament and seventy-one times in the King James Version Old Testament.

While there are a variety of words in the original languages that are translated by these English words, there are two that are significant for our study—*olam* in Hebrew and *aionios* in Greek—both of which have essentially the same meaning. They are also the words most often used to convey the thought of so-called never-ending time in our English-language Bibles.

The root meanings and most common uses of these words give us insight into how they were understood by the Bible writers. Neither of these words carries the idea of never-ending time—except when

---

1. *(Oxford Languages, taken from the internet 7/24/23).*

used twice as a sort of compound construction, which will be considered shortly.

The Greek *aionios* is an adjective derived from its noun *aion*. The word *aion* is the source of the English word *eon*, which is most often rightly understood as an *age*.

We know of the *Ice Age*, the *Bronze Age*, the *Industrial Age*, and many other "ages," each of which spanned a duration of time until being superseded by another age.

Both *aion* and its derivative *aionios* carry this same basic meaning—a duration of time.

However, our teaching and understanding have been that 'eternal' means forever and ever, without an end. Based solely on the meaning of the words used, this is patently false. We can also see the lack of truth in such verses as Philemon 1:15:

> For this perhaps is why he was parted from
> you for a while, that you might have him
> back forever.

It should be obvious that neither Philemon nor Onesimus could live together for eternity as the word is commonly understood.

There are times when these words are used in reference to God, and this is the basis most people use for their understanding of the word's meaning. Yes, God is "eternal" in the sense that He is the self-existent One without beginning or end.

However, to take what applies uniquely to God and apply it to ourselves—who have been created with a beginning—is to do injustice to the word's essential meaning of *age-enduring*.

When the references to God—which are fewer in number than any others—are taken out of the equation, we see something quite different.

Our biggest problem comes from our various translations of the Bible.

Please do not misunderstand. I am grateful for our translations and the rich variety of understanding they provide. However, when people use different translations, confusion or conflict can sometimes arise.

A simple example is the word *world*, which translates from at least three different Greek words, each of which bears no similarity to the others. These words are *kosmos*, *oikoumenē*, and *aion*. Sometimes the word *world* is used even when there is no equivalent word in the original text.

For instance, Jesus said to them,

> "Truly, I say to you, in the new world, when
> the Son of Man will sit on his glorious
> throne, you who have followed me will
> also sit on twelve thrones, judging the
> twelve tribes of Israel." (Matthew 19:28)

Here, the word *world* translates the Greek word for *regeneration*. The English Standard Version adds a note to that effect—but how many people read the translation notes?

With each new translation of the Bible published, we gain additional insight into the possible meanings of a passage. This often occurs as a result of advances in archaeology and historical sociology, as we gain a clearer understanding of what the writers were saying to the people of their time.

We are not people of their time. Therefore, we do not think like people of their time. We think like people of our time.

Any study of language will reveal the gradual development of language and its meanings, which undergo many changes. Sometimes those changes result in meanings completely different from what existed before.

For instance, when my children were growing up in the 1970s and 1980s, the word "bad" had come to mean "good." Of course, one had to pay attention to inflection and context to gain the correct understanding.

The same is true for the word "gay," which once meant happy and carefree and now refers to homosexuality.

Therefore, for us in the twenty-first century to apply our modern understanding to a word from the first century is more than ridiculous. This does not mean that you cannot read your Bible without a Greek lexicon at your side. It does mean that you cannot build your doctrines or your theology on a simple reading of your favorite English translation.

We simply cannot apply our sense and definition of eternity to the words as translated in the Bible. It is often the case that translators do not indicate when a word is used in a double form rather than a single use.

The word *aion* and its adjectival derivative *aionios* are sometimes used together and sometimes used twice, as in *aionios to aionios*. In either case, we should not think of "time without end," because that is not how the ancients ever conceived of these words.

Remember, we are limited human beings, and the concept of an eternity without end is outside our finite grasp. What is truly being expressed is *time out of mind*. It is beyond the limits of our comprehension, but that does not mean *forever and ever, never to cease*.

The very phrase *"time without end"* is an oxymoron when used to describe eternity, because the nature of time is limitation.

Therefore, whenever you read the word *eternal* or something similar in your Bible, you should think *age-enduring*. How long is an age? It lasts for time out of mind—incomprehensible, but not unlimited.

It should also be noted that *eternal* does not always refer to quantity (as in duration), but also to quality, as previously mentioned in reference to God.

In Jesus' high-priestly prayer in the garden (John 17), He defines *eternal life* as knowing God and Jesus (verse 3). There is nothing in this passage about how to obtain eternal life, which is how it has most often been explained. Rather, it is a simple definition of eternal life—knowing God.

Knowing the Lord brings about a quality of life that was not known while living in darkness. Therefore, *eternal* is more properly understood as a matter of quality rather than quantity.

Those who know the Lord are not waiting until they die to receive eternal life. They are already the possessors of eternal life and are enjoying its benefits now.

Verdict: Fiction

The modern concept of eternity as an endless existence beyond the reach of time was never in the minds of the Bible writers or their original readers. It has always been understood as *age-enduring*, even though the boundaries of such ages are beyond our ability to define.

8

OBJECTION— UNIVERSALISM FLIES IN THE FACE OF HIS WORD

Fact or Fiction

Universalism is contrary to the Bible

Another common objection to the teaching of the restoration of all things has been given as:

Objection: "It flies in the face of His Word, which says the wages of sin is death. Claims (sic) that God will save everyone consigns sinners to Hell by giving them no reason to repent and embrace Jesus's sacrifice."

Kudos to the one who posted this objection, because they gave a supporting verse. Usually, I only get a general statement of "It goes against the Bible," with nothing to support the claim.

Two things are presented within this objection, which we would do well to address—

- The wages of sin is death
- Sinners have no reason to repent

In the previous chapter, I said that some of the teaching of restoration is based on the meaning of words from the original. This objection presents us with an opportunity to address another of those words—repentance.

REPENTANCE

The word "repentance" was first introduced into our language in the fourteenth century, during the Middle English period. The English meaning of "be sorry for" has not changed over the centuries.

Interestingly, of the fifty-seven times that repent or repentance is used in the Bible, we are never once told what it is. We only read that it is necessary. We only have the concept of being sorry for our sins because that is what we have been taught.

We have once again applied our modern understanding to an ancient concept, neither of which has any similarity to the other.

The Hebrew word so translated means "to turn back," with the idea of returning to the starting place.

This thought reminds me of the church at Ephesus in Revelation, which was accused of having forsaken its first love.

> Remember therefore from where you have
> fallen; repent, and do the works you did at
> first. If not, I will come to you and
> remove your lampstand from its place,
> unless you repent. (Revelation 2:5)

The church is told to return to its first love, which would require repentance.

The Greek word translated as *repent/repentance* is *metanoia*, a compound word. *Meta* means "with," and *noia* means "mind" or "thought." Translated as *repent*, it simply means to change your mind.

To be sure, sometimes changing our minds is the result of feeling badly about something, but that is not the requirement for repentance. It is not necessary to "admit that you are a sinner" in order to repent.

We see this exemplified in Paul's second letter to the Corinthians.

> For godly grief produces a repentance that
> leads to salvation without regret, whereas
> worldly grief produces death. (2
> Corinthians 7:10)

It should be clear from this verse that the grief, the sorrow, is not the repentance, but that which produces the repentance. It produces a change of mind which brings about a change in life.

When an alcoholic decides he needs to quit drinking and does so, he has repented of his drinking. He hasn't acknowledged God, hasn't confessed any sin, hasn't prayed a prayer, but he has repented. In this instance, "salvation" is not a part of the equation, other than being saved from a tortured life.

Most teaching about salvation is that repentance is required in order to be saved. Isn't that putting the cart before the horse? I know many people who came to the Lord without admitting anything more than that they needed help. When they turned to the Lord for that help, their life began to change.

One of the clearest examples of repentance as changing your mind is found in the book of Hebrews, which speaks about Esau.

> "For you know that afterward, when he
> desired to inherit the blessing, he was
> rejected, for he found no chance to
> repent, though he sought it with tears."
> (Hebrews 12:17)

Esau had the tears. He had the sorrow. But he was rejected from receiving the blessing of the firstborn. He was not able to turn back and redo what had already been done. He was not able to repent.

As one who believes in the ultimate restoration of all things to their original condition, I accept the concept of repentance. I just do not accept it as a requirement for salvation. I recognize repentance as a fruit of salvation.

WAGES OF SIN

The implication of the person's objection to the inclusion of all in God's plan of salvation is that inclusion completely ignores sin and its consequences.

Once again, that is not true. The objection is based solely on a biased logic which assumes that the only reason for "getting saved" is to avoid hell, and that hell is only avoided by not sinning.

This faulty logic, therefore, assumes that a person who hears "God saves everyone" will then decide, "What's the point of being good, if everyone is saved in the end?" Surely you can see the "salvation by works" in that rationale.

Supposedly, all three of the major schools of theology—Arminianism, Calvinism, and Universalism—believe in salvation by grace through faith. If we truly believe that, then we wouldn't have this particular objection to the Universalist's theology. Other objections, maybe—but not this one.

Notice that the person's reasoning is that, in ignoring sin, the teaching causes people to go to hell because they have no reason to repent. Hopefully, the idea of repenting has been settled, but there is still the issue of sin and whether it is part of the teaching of inclusion of all.

Sin and its consequences are very much a part of a consistent theology, regardless of the particular school of thinking.

OBJECTION—UNIVERSALISM FLIES IN THE FACE OF HIS... 85

The verse quoted by the objector is, *"For the wages of sin is death, but the free gift of God is eternal life in Christ Jesus our Lord."* (Romans 6:23). Notice that "death" is your payment for committing sin. You **earn** death. However, there is no wage—no payment for something earned—to gain eternal life. It is the gift of God.

Most folks believe that the "free gift" must be taken or received, and if not, then there is no eternal life. This reasoning is only partly true. It assumes a "one-and-done" approach to salvation. If you don't do it in this life, then you are lost for all eternity. Maybe. Maybe not.

There is a companion verse to Romans 6:23 which almost every Christian can quote:

> "For all have sinned and fall short of the
>   glory of God." (Romans 3:23)

These two verses are often used when trying to present the gospel to someone. The modern evangelist wants to convince the person of their sinfulness and their need to repent and ask God for forgiveness. This has been the case as it has been taught for the past century. However, there is more to it than that.

Why have we never been told to read verse 24 of that passage?

> "And are justified by his grace as a gift,
>   through the redemption that is in Christ
>   Jesus." (Romans 3:24)

Let's read them both together:

> "For all have sinned and fall short of the
>   glory of God, and are justified by his
>   grace as a gift, through the redemption
>   that is in Christ Jesus." (Romans 3:23–24)

Who is it that is justified by His grace as a gift? Is it not the same "all" as those who have sinned? A simple understanding of the

English language should reveal that truth. *All have sinned, and all are justified.*

Now we are left with a real problem concerning the objection under consideration. If everyone has been justified from their sin, then how does sin "unjustify" someone? I cannot find that concept presented even once in the Bible.

Let's look at another verse which informs the Universalist understanding of sin and its consequences: "In Christ God was reconciling the world to himself, not counting their trespasses against them, and entrusting to us the message of reconciliation." (2 Corinthians 5:19)

God does not count the world's trespasses against them. The **only** way to dance around this verse is to say that "trespasses" does not mean sin. Since we all know that is not true, I would not argue with anyone who would try to make that distinction. I would leave them in their darkness.

The final verse in that passage from 2 Corinthians helps us to understand how God is able not to count our sins against us:

> "For our sake he made him to be sin who
> knew no sin, so that in him we might
> become the righteousness of God." (2
> Corinthians 5:21)

A Universalist understanding of salvation does not ignore sin and its consequences, but simply puts sin in its proper perspective.

Verdict: Fiction

Universalism has much support from the Bible and is able to explain most of the verses used as 'proof' against it.

9
HELL

Hell is a real place mentioned often in the Bible

If everyone is to be saved as a part of God's plan, and that saving is subject to His timing, then what about those who die without having accepted Jesus as their Savior?

This question is based on one of the major objections to the inclusion of all people in God's plan for salvation. Even though we have already looked at the true meaning of "forever" (Chapter Seven), there remains the problem of **hell**.

Most people believe that if you die without having confessed Jesus, you will go to hell. These same people also believe that hell is eternal—that one will burn forever in a place called hell. That burning is commonly described as *eternal conscious torment* for not having believed in Jesus.

Before we continue, let us consider a response to the objection of hell.

Would you not agree that the idea of infinite conscious torture after death would warrant the loudest, clearest, brightest, and simplest warning possible by God in the Bible?

And would you also agree that if there were such a horrendously gruesome fate awaiting the vast majority of people, the warning of it would need to appear at the earliest possible point—such as during creation week or immediately afterward?

If you agree to these premises, then I ask you to locate where a clear, loud, overt warning is given concerning the creation of such a place—and where this appears in the Bible. (I do not have the time to wait for you to locate that which is non-existent, so I will continue.)

What is hell?
Where is hell located?
What do we really know about hell?

Most of our concepts of this place come from paintings, books, and visions. There is no detailed description of hell given in the Bible. Much of what we believe today is derived from a fourteenth-century epic poem, *The Divine Comedy*, by Dante Alighieri.

The word *comedy* in the fourteenth century did not mean what it does today. It referred to a medieval narrative written with a hopeful or resolved ending.

The poem is written in three parts: *Inferno*, *Purgatorio*, and *Paradiso*. These Italian words translate as *Hell*, *Purgatory*, and *Paradise*. It is Dante's journey through the *Inferno*, escorted by the poet Virgil, from which we derive many of our mental images of what hell supposedly looks like.

> "In the poem, Hell is depicted as nine concentric circles of torment located within the Earth; it is the 'realm ... of those who have rejected spiritual values by yielding to bestial appetites or violence,

or by perverting their human intellect to fraud or malice against their fellow men."[1]

Obviously, the doctrine of hell existed long before the fourteenth century.

> "But it was Augustine of Hippo and his book *The City of God*, published in A.D. 426, that set the tone for official doctrine over the next 1,500 years. Hell existed not to reform or deter sinners, he argued. Its primary purpose was to satisfy the demands of justice. Augustine believed in the literal existence of a lake of fire, where 'by a miracle of their most omnipotent Creator, [the damned] can burn without being consumed, and suffer without dying.'"[2]

Prior to Augustine's time, there is no record of any of the Church Fathers holding such a doctrine of eternal conscious torment. Many believed in the soul's annihilation for those who died without Christ. Many also believed, as Augustine noted and objected to, that hell was a place for the reformation of sinners.

Why is the idea of the "reformation of sinners" unacceptable to most?

Surely there is biblical "proof" for hell, is there not? Those who espouse the doctrine have their Scripture verses always at the ready, saying, "The Bible clearly teaches that there is a hell." Augustine had his "proof" from the Latin Vulgate, published about the same time he wrote his famous *City of God*.

For the sake of argument, let us agree that the Bible "clearly teaches

1. *(quote taken from the internet 2/15/21. [https://en.wikipedia.org/wiki/Inferno_(Dante)])*
2. (quote taken from the internet 2/15/21— [https://www.nationalgeographic.com/news/2016/05/160513-theology-hell-history-christianity/#:~:text=St.,over%20the%20next%201%2C500%20years.&text=But%20it%20was%20Augustine%20of,or%20deter%20sinners%2C%20he%20argued.]) {*Use "Augustine of Hippo" as keyword search*}

that there is a hell." However, what most believe about hell is that it is a place where God tortures His creation forever and ever.

Is this proof, then? Well, maybe. Maybe not.

The word "hell" appears fifty-four times in the King James Version (KJV) in both the Old Testament and the New Testament. This is where most of our current biblical "proof" for the existence of hell comes from. Modern translations, however, contain only between thirteen and seventeen occurrences, all of which appear in the New Testament.

Why is there such a difference?
Could it be that what we have been taught is more hellish than hell itself?

It is important to know that **any translation is an interpretation**. The translators are certainly scholars far beyond my own abilities, yet they, too, bring preconceived ideas. They are, after all, human.

The difference has occurred due to greater linguistic knowledge of the ancient languages. That is the basis for translation work in its entirety. More translations continue to emerge as we gain a greater understanding of ancient thought.

Much of this new knowledge is not based solely on words, but on an expanded understanding of the times in which the Bible was written. This is key to making sense of any part of Scripture, not just the teaching on hell.

If we build our understanding solely on our knowledge of English, we will miss much of what was intended by the writers of Scripture. Not only will we miss much, but we will also likely misinterpret much. The English language is an ever-changing, living tongue, and even the meanings and uses of words change over time.

As mentioned in Chapter Seven, I recall when the word *gay* referred to happy and carefree times, such as "the gay nineties," referring to the end of the nineteenth century. Today, the word *gay* is used almost exclusively to indicate homosexuality.

Therefore, the differences between the KJV and modern translations in the use of the word "hell" have come about through changes in our language as well as a better understanding of ancient times and ancient words.

As previously stated, in the KJV, the word "hell" is used 54 times and appears in both the Old and New Testaments. In the English Standard Version (ESV), the word appears fourteen times, all in the New Testament.

Another striking biblical fact is the number of times hell is mentioned compared to other words we also deem important. In the KJV, *heaven* appears 582 times; *evil*, 613 times; *death*, 372 times; *sin*, 448 times; and *judgment*, 294 times. The ESV, of course, differs somewhat in the number of occurrences.

If hell is used only fifty-four times in the KJV, while these other words appear more than two hundred times each, should that disparity not raise a warning flag? Is hell really as central as it has been made out to be? Have we possibly made a mountain out of a molehill?

There are four words in the Bible translated as *hell* in the KJV: *sheol*, *hades*, *gehenna*, and *tartarus*.

Sheol

Sheol, which is Hebrew, is the only word in the Old Testament translated this way. It is rendered as *hell* thirty-one times, *grave* thirty-one times, and *pit* three times. According to Gesenius' *Hebrew-Chaldee Lexicon*, its basic meaning is that of a hollow in the ground—hence, *grave*.

Hell is often described as a place without God, meant to indicate the extreme loss experienced by those who end up there. However, *sheol* is used in this verse:

> If I ascend to heaven, You are there;
> If I make my bed in hell, behold, You are
>   there. (Psalm 139:8, KJV)

Therefore, hell cannot be a place where God is absent. Moreover, most evangelicals affirm the omnipresence of God. *Omnipresence* simply means "present everywhere." God is also present in the grave —or in hell, if one prefers that terminology.

The Septuagint (**LXX**), a Greek translation of the Old Testament produced approximately 250 years before Christ, uses the word *hades* for the Hebrew *sheol*.

Hades

The word *hades* appears eleven times in the KJV Greek concordance of the New Testament. This ancient Greek term has an interesting history. It has always been associated with the afterlife, though views concerning that afterlife evolved over time.

By the time of Jesus, a third view was emerging. Jesus "…knows the second conception, according to which the souls of the righteous are in the underworld as well as those of the ungodly (Luke 16:23, 26), and yet is also familiar with the third conception now in the process of emergence—namely, that the souls of the righteous are in Paradise (Luke 16:9, 23, 43)."[3]

Therefore, in Jesus' time, there was an amalgamation of two historical concepts associated with the word *hades*: "On the one side, in accordance with the older view, it denotes the whole sphere of the

---

3. *(Theological Dictionary of the New Testament, vol 1, pg 147, Gerhard Kittel)*

dead; on the other, it denotes only the temporary sojourn of the souls of the ungodly."[4]

This idea of hell being only temporary must have carried through for a few centuries, as we saw from Augustine's comments.

In the time of Jesus, *hades* was understood to be temporary. However, since—and largely because of—Augustine, it has come to be viewed as eternal, or forever. Since Jesus never made this plain Himself, what are we to believe?

If we translate *hades* as hell, with the idea of a place of eternal conscious torment in flames of fire for the unrighteous, we are left with an extremely thorny problem in the book of Revelation:

> Then Death and Hades were thrown into the
> lake of fire. This is the second death, the
> lake of fire. (Revelation 20:14)

The lake of fire has been taught as a descriptor of hell, and *hades* is the Greek word translated *hell*. What we see, then, is that hell is cast into hell. I know there are many things in the book of Revelation that appear confusing, but this borders on the absurd if we remain with the common understanding of hell.

What is plain is that Jesus never spoke of hell in a descriptive way or as a place to fear. The word *hades* appears only four times in the Gospels, and two of those occurrences are the same story recorded by different evangelists. Therefore, Jesus uses the word only three times.

None of those uses gives any indication of eternity in that place. The parable of the Rich Man and Lazarus includes the word *torment* in reference to being in *hades*, but nothing is said about the length of time.

---

4. (*ibid*)

Tartarus

Another word translated as *hell* is *tartarus*, found only once in 2 Peter 2:4. Notice that Peter frames the term as temporary:

> "For if God did not spare angels when they
> sinned, but cast them into hell and
> committed them to chains of gloomy
> darkness **to be kept until the
> judgment**..."

They are kept for a period of time—*until*. They are apparently then released, and something else happens to them.

Up to this point, much of what we have seen could be dismissed as interpretation or speculation. The final word, however, removes all doubt. It not only demonstrates the temporary nature of hell, but also calls its very existence into question.

Gehenna

That word is *Gehenna*.

Gehenna appears twelve times in the New Testament—eleven times in the Gospels and once in James. Gehenna was originally the Valley of Hinnom, located south of Jerusalem, where refuse and dead animals from the city were discarded and burned.

These fires burned continuously because they were constantly fueled, which gave rise to the idea of "forever." However, they are not burning today. Jesus spoke of the wicked being sent to a place called *Gehenna*, but He never mentioned forever or anything related to its duration. James likewise makes no reference to duration in his use of the term (James 3:6).

There is one passage where the interpretation of "forever" is often introduced:

> And if your hand causes you to sin, cut it off.
> It is better for you to enter life crippled
> than with two hands to go to hell, to the
> unquenchable fire. (Mark 9:43)

The word *unquenchable* may seem to imply perpetuity. However, this word translated *unquenchable* appears only three times in the New Testament and reflects the natural condition of the fires of *Gehenna* —fires that did not burn out because they were continually fueled with dead bodies.

In fact, every reference to *Gehenna* includes the body. Some include the soul, but **none** include the spirit of man. This should not surprise us, because:

> ...the dust returns to the earth as it was, and
> the spirit returns to God who gave it.
> (Ecclesiastes 12:7)

Have you never considered the incongruity of a physical body burning for all eternity?

Sadly, *Gehenna* is translated as hell, but that is not what Jesus said. He said *Gehenna*. The word hell entered later as an interpretive choice, first appearing in the Latin Vulgate, as shown earlier.

When Jesus declared the purpose of His ministry (Luke 4:18), when He sent the disciples out to preach (Matthew 10:5), and when He gave the so-called Great Commission (Matthew 28:19), He never mentioned hell. He did not instruct them to frighten people with the prospect of dying and going there. He did not tell them to emphasize sin. Everything He proclaimed was **good news**—and there is no bad news in the good news.

Does it not raise concern that neither Jesus, Paul, nor any of the other New Testament writers ever speak of an "urgent necessity" to save people from hell? None of them mentions this idea when discussing the gospel or evangelism. If the ultimate goal—as many believe—is to save people from hell, would it not make sense that this would be included in the New Testament?

With all this being said, we are still left with the original question:
What about those who die without having accepted Jesus as their Savior?
What happens to them?

They probably go to the place we consider hell, but let us not put hell and eternity together in the same thought. As Augustine pointed out, hell was once believed to be a temporary place for the soul to be reformed.

If "reformation" is the purpose, then there is obviously a limited length of time. That time is limited to however long it takes for the soul to be reformed.

Using the word eternity as a descriptor for the time in hell reveals a major injustice—even by our human standards.

What punishment should last forever?
How can that serve any purpose?

Given the short span of the human life—seventy years, or a few more—how is an eternal punishment any kind of justice by comparison?

The most we can give a hardened, vicious criminal is life in prison—and then it is done.

How is it conceivable that God, in His mercy, in His love, would sentence a frail human who has never heard the gospel to an eternity of flames?

I believe it should be quite obvious that we have added our own tendency toward vindictiveness to the concept of hell and made that to be what God is like.

How to reconcile the common understanding of hell with "God is love" is beyond the capability of my limited thinking.

Verdict: Fact AND fiction

Hell may be a real place, but is not often mentioned in the Bible.

10

OBJECTION—JUDGMENT

Fact or Fiction

The biblical concept of judgment refers to hell and eternity

Another objection I received is, "Throughout Scripture, judgment exists. Jesus spoke of it ('Depart from Me, I never knew you, you who practice lawlessness'… Matthew 7:23) [sic], and the Spirit of the Lord spoke to John through his revelatory vision, laying out the end of this realm. Judgment is separation from God if the Scripture is to be believed."

This is the common understanding of judgment as presented to most believers—what they believe the Bible teaches. Notice, however, that this person did not explicitly include eternity in their thoughts; it is implied.

As pointed out in the previous chapter, the word "judgment" appears in the King James Version (KJV) 294 times. In the English Standard Version (ESV), it is used 170 times. This disparity is due to modern translations having a better understanding of ancient languages, coupled with the discovery of ancient manuscripts not available to the translators of the KJV.

Obviously, it is not possible to consider every single use of the word in the Bible, but I will give it some consideration for your understanding.

The first occurrence of the word judgment is found in Genesis:

> "But I will bring judgment on the nation that
> they serve, and afterward they shall come
> out with great possessions" (Genesis
> 15:14).

This translates the Hebrew word *din* (Strong's H1777). It is used 24 times and is most often translated as 'judge'.

Interestingly, it is used in a negative sense only 3 times (Genesis 15:14; 1 Samuel 2:10; Psalm 110:6). In the remaining 21 occurrences, it is used positively, as when Rachel expresses gratitude for the birth of her son:

> "Then Rachel said, 'God has judged me, and
> has also heard my voice and given me a
> son.' Therefore she called his name Dan"
> (Genesis 30:6)

In the verses from 1 Samuel and Psalms, the judgment is temporal. There is nothing said about an eternity of torture or destruction in any of the 24 occurrences of this Hebrew word.

The next word translated as *judgment* is the Hebrew word *shephet* (Strong's H8201), which appears 16 times. Its first appearance is in Exodus:

> "Say therefore to the people of Israel, 'I am
> the LORD, and I will bring you out from
> under the burdens of the Egyptians, and I
> will deliver you from slavery to them, and
> I will redeem you with an outstretched

arm and with great acts of judgment'"
(Exodus 6:6)

We know from the narrative that these judgments were all physical. There is nothing about the Egyptians who died spending an eternity in hell as a result of their treatment of God's people.

All remaining uses of this word convey physical judgment within this realm of life. This is vividly portrayed in Ezekiel:

> "For thus says the Lord GOD: How much
> more when I send upon Jerusalem my four
> disastrous acts of judgment—sword,
> famine, wild beasts, and pestilence—to cut
> off from it man and beast!" (Ezekiel 14:21)

Again, there is no thought of eternity attached to these judgments.

The next word is *mishpat* (Strong's H4941), which is used 421 times. Its first occurrence is also in Genesis:

> "For I have chosen him, that he may
> command his children and his household
> after him to keep the way of the LORD
> by doing righteousness and justice, so that
> the LORD may bring to Abraham what
> he has promised him" (Genesis 18:19)

Here it is translated as *justice*.

While the word is translated in a variety of ways, judgment is by far the most common rendering, appearing 296 times. The idea conveyed is that of judging between two things—what we might call discernment.

For example, when buying a piece of fruit, one judges between options to determine which is best. This is the basic idea of *mishpat*.

These are all the Hebrew words translated as *judgment* in the Old Testament. We can see that judgment is never associated with the afterlife or eternity. It **always** refers to something that occurs in this life, both positive and negative.

Stated plainly, the judgments of God in the Old Testament always involve some form of temporal action—punishment, destruction, or removal—within this world.

In the New Testament, the word "judgment" appears 76 times in the KJV and 73 times in the ESV. The Greek word *krisis* (Strong's G2920) is most commonly used, appearing 48 times. Other words translated as *judgment* convey different meanings and derive from different Greek terms, such as Paul's opinion in 1 Corinthians 7:25 and the judgment seat in 2 Corinthians 5:10.

The first occurrence of *krisis* appears in Matthew's account of the Sermon on the Mount:

> "You have heard that it was said to those of
>   old, 'You shall not murder; and whoever
>   murders will be liable to judgment'"
> (Matthew 5:21)

Jesus does not define the judgment here. It is only our interpretation that assumes this refers to going to hell. In the following verse, however, Jesus clarifies the concept of murder and states that calling someone a "fool" puts one in danger of "hellfire." Here, *hell* is a translation of the Greek word *Gehenna* (see Chapter 9). Still, nothing in the text itself suggests an eternal outcome.

Since Jesus was addressing Jews, He was referring to their law concerning murder and its consequences: *"Whoever kills an animal shall make it good, and whoever kills a person shall be put to death"* (Leviticus 24:21). The Law addressed accidental killing, negligence, ignorance, and premeditation—but none of these involved an eternity separated from God. Judgment was always temporal and physical.

Most uses of *krisis* follow this same pattern of discernment—making distinctions or judgments between things:

> "Do not judge by appearances, but judge
> with right judgment" (John 7:24)

However, when the phrase *day of judgment* is used, it refers to something occurring after earthly life:

> "And just as it is appointed for man to die
> once, and after that comes judgment"
> (Hebrews 9:27)

FUTURE JUDGMENT

Another passage associates this future judgment with destruction rather than eternal torment:

> "But by the same word the heavens and earth
> that now exist are stored up for fire, being
> kept until the day of judgment and
> destruction of the ungodly" (2 Peter 3:7)

Even here, there is no explicit connection between judgment, hell, and eternity. Almost all biblical uses of judgment concern events within this realm, except for the *day of judgment*, which occurs afterward.

This phrase appears only seven times, all in the New Testament.

Many books have been written on judgment—especially the Day of Judgment—but nearly all of them speculate that hell is the result, despite no explicit biblical statement to that effect.

Finally, let's consider the verse cited by the original objector:

> "And then will I declare to them, 'I never
> knew you; depart from me, you workers
> of lawlessness'" (Matthew 7:23)

Again, it should be obvious that interpreting this as eternal separation in hell is an assumption. The passage itself says nothing of the sort. Let's put it in its context.

This statement appears at the conclusion of the Sermon on the Mount.

> "Not everyone who says to me, 'Lord, Lord,'
> will enter the kingdom of heaven... And
> then will I declare to them, 'I never knew
> you; depart from me, you workers of
> lawlessness'" (Matthew 7:21-23)

The most fascinating aspect of this passage is who Jesus addresses—religious people doing religious things apart from knowing the Truth.

This is not a rebuke of overtly wicked people doing wicked things, though it is often preached that way.

Jesus uses the phrase "on that day," which many interpret as the Day of Judgment. There is nothing in the passage itself that specifies when "that day" occurs, nor does Jesus attach to it any reference to eternal punishment or hell.

The Greek word translated *depart* appears only three times in the New Testament.

In the other two occurrences, it clearly denotes a temporary separation rather than a final or eternal one.

THE JUDGMENT SEAT OF CHRIST

There are two major views among many evangelicals concerning future judgment: the Bema Seat and the Great White Throne.

The Bema Seat refers to two verses from Paul in which he uses the Greek word *bēma*—Romans 14:10 and 2 Corinthians 5:10. In both instances, the word is translated as *the judgment seat.*

The common teaching is that the Bema Seat judgment is for believers only. However, in both verses, Paul says "we…all," without making a distinction. For the sake of argument, though, I will grant the interpretation that this judgment applies only to believers. Even so, in neither verse is there any indication of a prolonged period of time associated with either reward or punishment.

The Great White Throne is mentioned only once, in Revelation 20:11. The claim is often made that this judgment applies only to unbelievers. However, if the entire passage from verses 11 through 15 is considered, it is difficult to maintain that believers are excluded.

The idea that this judgment concerns unbelievers only is taken from verse 15: "And if anyone's name was not found written in the book of life, he was thrown into the lake of fire." It should be noted, however, that until verse 15, those being judged are identified simply as "the dead":

> And I saw the dead, great and small, standing
> before the throne, and books were
> opened. Then another book was opened,
> which is the book of life. And the dead
> were judged by what was written in the
> books, according to what they had done.
> And the sea gave up the dead who were
> in it, Death and Hades gave up the dead

> who were in them, and they were judged,
> each one of them, according to what they
> had done. (Revelation 20:12–13)

The text states that "the dead were judged...according to what they had done." Is this not the same thought expressed in 2 Corinthians 5:10?

> "For we must all appear before the judgment
> seat of Christ, so that each one may
> receive what is due for what he has done
> in the body, whether good or evil."

Attempting to make a sharp distinction between these two judgments is more challenging than simply "splitting hairs."

For those who claim to take the Bible literally and to believe only what is revealed in Scripture, I find this approach disconcerting. Much has been added to the text, yet those who accept these passages as they stand are often accused of adding to the Word of God.

Perhaps it is time to begin rereading the Bible without the doctrinal filters imposed by centuries of speculation.

Verdict: Fiction

Never once is judgment associated with hell or eternity in the entirety of Scripture.

11

OBJECTION—
GOD IS JUST

Fact or Fiction: God is just and His justice demands punishment for sin

Whenever I speak with someone about God's love for all—whether they are unfamiliar with the concept or knowingly object to the idea of salvation for all—the most common response I hear is, "Yes, but God is also just."

What does that mean? And why is it so often introduced with a "Yes, but…"?

The word "but" is a conjunction that negates everything that precedes it. The "yes" functions merely as a conciliatory word, used to soften the objection that follows. It seems many people employ this response without fully comprehending its implications.

Essentially, the objection asserts that justice is more necessary than love—or that justice is primary in God's nature or plan. In my experience, the latter is more often the case. Many have come to believe that the sole reason God placed humanity here was to test whether we would truly love Him. If we fail that test, then God has a furnace prepared for those who do not pass.

(Hogwash!)

JUSTICE

Before we consider any of the Bible verses under this topic, let us examine our concept and understanding of "justice." In order to fully grasp the nature of God's justice, we should first consider the English meaning of the word and the family of words associated with it—*just, justified, justifier,* and *justification.* As a word family, they all originate from the same basic meaning.

As far back as the Greek philosophers—Plato and Aristotle—the notion of justice involved each thing existing within its proper sphere or serving its proper purpose. The idea of inequality in aptitude and outcome is clearly implied. Stated simply, we are all equal in the eyes of God, but we are not all equal in function or ability.

This concept appears in Paul's letter to the Corinthians:

> Are all apostles? Are all prophets? Are all
> teachers? Do all work miracles? Do all
> possess gifts of healing? Do all speak with
> tongues? Do all interpret? (1 Corinthians
> 12:29–30)

These are rhetorical questions with the obvious answer of no. Not everyone possesses any one particular gift, nor does any individual possess all of the gifts. Each gift places a person in a position of "inequality" relative to those who do not possess it. Nothing is said about a hierarchy of gifts—about one being more important than another—except for love, which everyone is encouraged to pursue.

The English word "justice" comes from Old French and carries several related meanings. The two primary senses were *uprightness* and *equity.* This understanding is not about *making* things right through punishment, but about things *being* right—existing in proper order.

It was not until the middle of the fifteenth century that English usage adopted a legal sense of justice associated with vindictive punishment. The idea of punishment for a wrong committed against another is certainly present in the Bible, particularly within the Law of Moses (Exodus 21:22-27; Leviticus 24:19-20). However, Jesus turned this concept on its head in the Sermon on the Mount:

> "You have heard that it was said, 'An eye for
> an eye and a tooth for a tooth.' But I say
> to you…" (Matthew 5:38–39a)

Most societies today still operate from the framework established in the Law of Moses. We hear it expressed whenever a wrong is committed: "I want justice for what he did. He should pay." The meaning is clear—punishment should be inflicted on the one who committed the offense, and this is what we commonly call justice.

This way of thinking has become so deeply ingrained, after centuries of use, that it may be difficult for us to imagine any alternative understanding. Yet, if we truly want to understand the justice of God, we must be willing to reconsider it.

The granddaddy of most English Bible translations is the King James Version, first published in 1611, at the beginning of the seventeenth century. By that time, English law had been using the concept of vindictive punishment within the word "justice" for approximately 200 years. This prolonged usage firmly established that meaning in the minds of the people.

That inherited meaning is now the concept many apply to God's justice. We have taken what is true within our legal systems and projected it onto God Himself. In doing so, we have allowed English translations of Scripture to shape our understanding more than the Hebrew meanings underlying the text.

One might ask, "Isn't 'an eye for an eye' justice? Doesn't that confirm the common meaning of the word?"

No. That is simply circular reasoning.

JUST

The word "just" is the primary term in this word family and requires careful explanation, since our understanding of *justice, justified, justifier,* and *justification* hinges on it. Justice is the noun from which the adjective "just" comes. Since the argument against God's universal love for all is based on the phrase "God is just," it is necessary that we explore that meaning. We cannot simply apply our limited English meaning of punishment without also understanding the Hebrew meaning.

The Hebrew word (צֶדֶק *sedeq;* Strong's H6664) is used 119 times in the Old Testament with the basic meaning of rightness, or straightness. From this, the concept of equality naturally follows, as illustrated in Leviticus 19:35-36:

> You shall do no wrong in judgment, in
>   measures of length or weight or quantity.
>   You shall have just balances, just weights,
>   a just ephah, and a just hin: I am the
>   LORD your God, who brought you out
>   of the land of Egypt.

Your standard of measure is to be equal in all things at all times. A one-ounce weight is to be one ounce, not 1.1 ounces. On a balance scale, a 1.1-ounce weight would require a little more product to balance, but it would only be called one ounce. That is cheating.

Can we apply this concept to God and His dealings with humanity? Not only can we, but we should. His dealings with us are equitable. He treats us all the same.

This is where it gets tricky, maybe even sticky.

We subscribe to the idea that no one is above the law. Everyone is to be treated the same under the same law. That is good and equitable, and there is no argument as to its meaning and application.

When the law says that to commit murder is punishable by death of the murderer, then anyone and everyone who commits murder should die. That is equity.

When we say God is just in this light, then we would expect that all who do the same wrong will be punished the same way.

However, using the word just to describe someone's character sometimes includes our idea of mercy. For instance, consider Matthew 1:19: "And her husband Joseph, being a just man and unwilling to put her to shame, resolved to divorce her quietly."

Uprightness, righteousness, equity, and straightness each point more to the person who has these qualities than to someone who demands "an eye for an eye." Being just, then, is an earmark of a higher quality than the mere human notion of vindication or vengeance.

Would you not agree that God is of a higher moral character than we?

Let us not lower God's character to our level, but let us try to rise to the higher standard to which He has called us. Our concept of raw, bare-bones justice demands punishment—"an eye for an eye."

> But I say to you, Do not resist the one who is
>   evil. But if anyone slaps you on the right
>   cheek, turn to him the other also.
>   (Matthew 5:39)

If Jesus requires this of us, then why do we think that the Father does differently?

If we are called to love our enemies (Matthew 5:44), should we not expect the same from God?

Jesus continually pointed out how our human nature, in line with the Law of Moses, was not the higher standard by which God operated. Jesus has called us to rise to that higher standard.

> You therefore must be perfect, as your
> heavenly Father is perfect. (Matthew
> 5:48)

So far, we have considered justice and seen that we have applied only an English, legal understanding to the idea of God's justice. We have also looked at the word "just" and seen that it means much more than simply deciding who gets what kind of punishment. Let's turn our attention now to the word justify.

JUSTIFY

The theological definition is to make righteous before God. None of us has a problem with that. Our differences lie in how one is made righteous. The Jews, of course, believed that righteousness came through keeping the Law. Many Christians today still believe somewhat the same thing.

While they believe that we become Christians—that is, "get saved" —by faith in Jesus, which makes us righteous, many think that righteousness is maintained by doing what is right. Righteousness is a state of being, not a way of life.

Another meaning of the word is to show something to be right or reasonable. For instance, "Our confidence in you has been fully justified by your exceptional skills."

There is another use of the word justify that more readily illustrates its meaning. It comes from the printing industry, where text is justified by filling the space between the margins equally.

The concept of equity, or equality, is once again demonstrated as a meaning within this word family.

Consider Romans 3:26:

> It was to show his righteousness at the present
> time, so that he might be just and the
> justifier of the one who has faith in Jesus.

Both *just* and *justifier* are used in this single sentence.

The first thing to notice is that God is just, which is the objection under consideration. However, the emphasis here is not on meting out punishment but on demonstrating mercy.

God's mercy is what makes Him just.

James understood this when he wrote, "Mercy triumphs over judgment (James 2:13b)."

The objection focuses on the claim that God is just, while implying that punishment for sin is what makes Him just.

No. What makes God just is His mercy, just as was stated earlier concerning Mary's husband, Joseph.

If I take Romans 3:26 and allow it to stand completely by itself, out of context, then what I am saying may appear to be merely opinion. We all know, however, that any text without a context becomes a pretext for a proof-text. So let us look at the context. If your Bible is divided into sections or paragraphs, you will see that the passage spans verses 21-26.

Within this section, we find one of the most frequently quoted verses concerning the need for salvation: "for all have sinned and fall short of the glory of God" (Romans 3:23).

This verse is lifted completely out of its context so that the one doing the witnessing can convince the listener that he or she is a sinner. However, consider the verse that is almost never quoted alongside verse 23: "and are justified by his grace as a gift, through the redemption that is in Christ Jesus" (Romans 3:24).

We are justified as a gift.
We are declared not guilty as a gift.

We escape the penalty due for sin through the gift of grace.

That alone is remarkable. Yet what is so often overlooked is *for whom* this has been done. Certainly, we see ourselves included—but we are not the only ones.

Look again at the full statement: ALL have sinned and are justified. There is no legitimate way to restrict this to believers alone. Everyone sinned, and everyone is justified. Believers are simply those who are enjoying the benefits of His grace presently.

God is indeed just. In His justice, God has justified everyone who has ever sinned through the blood of Jesus Christ. My justification —and yours—rests on that fact alone.

Is God just? Absolutely.

Does that prove Universalism false? Not at all. In fact, the objection accomplishes the opposite. It supports God's desire, will, and plan to bring everyone to the saving knowledge of the Lord Jesus Christ.

Verdict: Fiction

God's justice is informed by His mercy toward sinners.

12
ALL

Fact or Fiction

ALL seldom means everyone.

At one time, my argument against the idea of all people being saved rested on the fact that *all* does not always mean *everyone*. For instance, in a few places in the Gospels, we read statements such as:

> "In those days, a decree went out from
>   Caesar Augustus that all the world should
>   be registered" (Luke 2:1).

Most people are comfortable understanding *all the world* to mean all the world known to the Roman Empire. It clearly does not mean "all the world in its entirety."

> And he taught in their synagogues, being
>   glorified by all. (Luke 4:15)

We know from other passages of Scripture that the scribes and Pharisees did not praise Him. Therefore, Jesus was not being glorified by *all* without exception.

> Early in the morning, he came again to the
> temple. All the people came to him, and
> he sat down and taught them. (John 8:2)

This is obviously not all people everywhere, but a limited group—namely, those present at the temple at that time.

> All who came before me are thieves and
> robbers, but the sheep did not listen to
> them. (John 10:8)

Here, even though Jesus is speaking, we know that not everyone who came before Him was a thief or a robber. He is clearly referring to "all of a class."

There were prophets whose writings remain and who do not belong in this category. In the time of Jesus, this would include figures such as Simeon and John the Baptist.

In these examples, *'all' does not necessarily mean 'all'* in every situation or usage of the term.

For me, this was enough to persuade me that the teaching that *all people will eventually be saved* was not correct.

However, an exception does not disprove the rule. A general rule does not have to be universally true in every situation in order to be valid; it is *generally* true, not universally so.

This distinction becomes important when we examine passages that cannot be interpreted as all of a class. For example, we believe that **all have sinned** and that **all died in Adam**.

This is not "all of a class"—it refers to all people of all time, across all nations.

Let us begin, then, with a section of Scripture that is seldom taught because it is often considered difficult to understand—Romans 5.

ALL AND MANY

Romans 5:12, 15, 18–19

> ^{12} Therefore, just as sin came into the world
> through one man, and death through sin,
> and so death spread to all men because all
> sinned…
>
> ^{15} But the free gift is not like the trespass. For
> if many died through one man's trespass,
> much more have the grace of God and
> the free gift by the grace of that one man,
> Jesus Christ, abounded for many…
>
> ^{18} Therefore, as one trespass led to
> condemnation for all men, so one act of
> righteousness leads to justification and life
> for all men.
>
> ^{19} For as by the one man's disobedience the
> many were made sinners, so by the one
> man's obedience the many will be made
> righteous.

The main reason this passage is not often taught is because of one verse that I did not initially include—verse 17. This verse is frequently preached, but rarely within the context of the surrounding verses.

> For if, because of one man's trespass, death
> reigned through that one man, much
> more will those who receive the
> abundance of grace and the free gift of
> righteousness reign in life through the one
> man Jesus Christ. (Romans 5:17)

This verse appears to indicate that only those who accept Jesus will have eternal life. Standing alone, without the broader context, that would seem to be the best interpretation.

Of course, this reflects the prevailing paradigm that is brought to this—and to nearly every other passage dealing with salvation or judgment. Each of us begins interpretation from within our existing framework of belief.

We have been so deeply conditioned to think that salvation requires "accepting Jesus" that it becomes difficult to see beyond that assumption. As a result, we often read into a passage something that may not actually be present.

This is one such case. *The plain statement is simply "those who receive."* It does not specify how they receive or what they must do. It only states that they receive.

When our limited English understanding is combined with this entrenched paradigm, the only interpretation that seems possible is that "those who receive" refers exclusively to those who willingly accept Jesus as their Savior.

We often illustrate this by saying that in order to receive a gift, one must extend a hand and accept it.

But is that the only way something can be received?

I received a cold virus last winter. I did not ask for it. I did not acknowledge its presence before it entered my body. My body simply received it.

This is admittedly a weak illustration, but it opens the door to another concept—one with which you will likely agree.

Consider the idea of direct deposit. If I had your bank account number and deposited one hundred dollars into your account, you did nothing to receive it. You did not know it was coming. I did it simply because I chose to. You received it.

Do you have to spend it? No.
Could you return it?
Yes.

But none of that changes the fact that you received it. It was given. That is the point—and we will return to this when we address objections to the idea that *all* truly means *all*.

Therefore, let's allow verse 17 to stand on its own without forcing it into our paradigm of belief.

If we insist on interpreting it according to that faulty system, then the surrounding verses become extremely difficult—if not impossible—to understand.

Verse 12

> Therefore, just as sin came into the world
>   through one man, and death through sin,
>   and so death spread to all men because all
>   sinned…

Adam sinned, and his sin brought death into the world. That death spread to all men because all sinned. This is fairly plain and straightforward.

We readily accept the idea that all people are born sinners because all trace their lineage back to Adam. Theologians refer to this as *the federal headship of Adam*.

Verses 13 and 14 compare sin and death in relation to Adam, Moses, and the Law. Then we come to verse 15.

Verse 15

> But the free gift is not like the trespass. For if
> many died through one man's trespass,
> much more have the grace of God and
> the free gift by the grace of that one man,
> Jesus Christ, abounded for many.

The free gift differs from the trespass in that the trespass earned death, while the gift requires no action in order to be given. Death was earned; the gift was not. That is precisely what makes it a gift.

One of the commonly cited "proofs" that salvation does not apply to everyone is found in the final phrase of this verse—"abounded for many." The word *many* is taken as evidence that salvation does not extend to all.

However, this interpretation does injustice to the rest of the verse, because *many* is also used to describe those who died as a result of Adam's trespass.

Are we to believe that only a select few died because of Adam's sin?

Certainly not, since the passage has already told us that death spread to all.

Therefore, we are compelled to conclude that the *many* for whom grace abounded is the same *many* for whom death came.

Verses 16 and 17 continue to compare and contrast the trespass and the gift, much like verses 13 and 14. Then Paul concludes his argument in verse 18.

Verse 18

> Therefore, as one trespass led to
> condemnation for all men, so one act of
> righteousness leads to justification and life
> for all men.

Paul's use of *therefore* signals that he is bringing his previous thoughts to a conclusion.

Because of Adam's sin, how many people were condemned? **All**. Because of Christ's act of righteousness, how many are led to justification and life? **All**.

The phrase *for all men* appears in the Greek text in exactly the same form in both clauses. The same words are used, in the same order, across the manuscript evidence.

There is no logical way to interpret one '*all*' as meaning everyone and the other as meaning only some. Doing so exceeds the bounds of reason and undermines the plain reading of the text. Paul reinforces this point directly in verse 19.

Verse 19

> For as by the one man's disobedience the
> many were made sinners, so by the one
> man's obedience the many will be made
> righteous.

Here, Paul makes no distinction between *all* and *many*. In verse 18, he uses *all*; in verse 19, continuing the same argument, he uses *many*.

It is not possible for a rational mind to separate the ones affected by Christ from the ones affected by Adam.

By one man's disobedience, *many* were made sinners.

By one man's obedience, *many* will be made righteous.

The phrase *the many* appears identically in both clauses. If we insist that the many made righteous refers only to some, then we must also conclude that only some were made sinners through Adam—an impossible conclusion.

Notice also that the verb *will be made righteous* is in the future tense, with no specified timeframe. It will happen. We may not know when, but it will happen.

Paul makes the same claim elsewhere:

> For as in Adam all die, so also in Christ all
> will be made alive. (1 Corinthians 15:22)

This verse is often preached as though it means one must get oneself "into Christ" before it is too late. But that interpretation is driven by doctrine, not by the text itself.

All in Adam is the same as *all* in Christ.
There is no distinction based on human action.

This understanding also clarifies something Jesus said:

> "And I, when I am lifted up from the earth,
> will draw all to myself." (John 12:32)

When read in isolation, this verse is often interpreted to mean that Jesus will draw people from all nations, not all people. But why could He not have said that explicitly if that is what He meant?

The Greek text includes neither *men* nor *people*. It simply reads *all*. The addition of *people* is interpretive, not translational, and not even a legitimate interpretation.

This interpretation is often challenged by experience—we do not see everyone coming to Jesus. Therefore, the conclusion is that He did not mean *all*.

When did our experience become the final authority for biblical truth?

John explains that Jesus was referring to the kind of death He would die (verse 33). His being lifted up refers to the crucifixion.

Notice first of all that Jesus did not give a time frame for that "drawing" of people to Himself. It is future tense, the same as the verse we looked at in Romans.

The Greek verb is in the future active indicative, indicating an ongoing action presented as certain. Thus, while you may have already been drawn, it does not mean your neighbor has been drawn. That remains in God's hands.

The word "draw" is also an interesting term. We often think of it as something akin to wooing a lover—gentle and non-coercive, without violating personal boundaries. However, that is not always the case.

The same Greek word is used for hauling a net of fish (John 21:6) and for dragging Paul and Silas into the marketplace (Acts 16:19).

Consider this usage. He said to them,

> "Cast the net on the right side of the boat,
>   and you will find some." So they cast it,
>   and now they were not able to haul it in,
>   because of the quantity of fish. (John 21:6)

No fisherman has ever tried to "woo" a net full of fish.

They haul it.
They drag it.

Or consider this verse:

> "But when her owners saw that their hope of
> gain was gone, they seized Paul and Silas
> and dragged them into the marketplace
> before the rulers." (Acts 16:19)

There is nothing gentle about the way Paul and Silas were treated. These two words—*haul* and *dragged*—are translated from the same Greek word rendered as "draw" in John 12:32.

Other verses also show the concept of *draw* as something more than gentle (SEE JOHN 21:11; ACTS 21:30; JAMES 2:6).

So, set aside the idea of gentleness as a function of human free will. People often say that God will not force Himself on anyone, which is true, but not because of our so-called free will. God will use whatever is necessary to help a person choose the right path. One is either drawn into the Kingdom or dragged in. And remember, the timing belongs to God, not to us.

John tells us something at the beginning of his Gospel that, on the surface, appears to elevate human free will as the decisive factor in salvation:

> "He came as a witness to bear witness about
> the light, that all might believe through
> him." (John 1:7)

The difficulty lies in the English word "might." When used as a verb, we tend to hear it as indicating mere possibility. For example, if I say, "I might go to the store later," I am expressing uncertainty, not a guaranteed outcome.

Left to our English instincts alone, that may seem like a reasonable way to read this verse. However, the Greek construction points not to possibility, but to certainty—a completed intention.

In other words, all will believe through Him—a point we will return to when we examine the use of *might* more fully.

Finally, we look at an important passage that uses the word "all," which also includes the word "desires" in reference to God's will.

> "Who desires all people to be saved and to
> come to the knowledge of the truth. For
> there is one God, and there is one
> mediator between God and men, the man
> Christ Jesus, who gave himself as a
> ransom for all, which is the testimony
> given at the proper time." (1 Timothy 2:4-
> 6)

Most people will gloss over the fact of the ransom being for all and try to shift the focus to the word "desires." The interpretation is that God only hopes that everyone will be saved. Poor God. He is limited by man's free will, which ultimately reigns supreme in all things.

A poor translation, a self-centered understanding, and a weak interpretation have misled us.

The Greek word used is *thelo*, which appears 210 times in the KJV and is translated in a variety of ways—will/would = 177 times, with the remainder being similar to desire.

> Greek scholar Gottlob Schrenk writes, "God's *thelo* is always characterized by absolute definiteness, sovereign self-assurance and efficacy. It is resolute and completely willing."[1]

It is a shame that our translators have inserted their biased belief into this verse, which renders God as a hapless being who is not able to achieve what He desires.

---

1. *(Theological Dictionary of New Testament Words edited by Gerhard Kittel. Vol III, pg 47)*

Using the verses shown, it should be impossible to continue thinking that Adam's transgression is more powerful than Christ's obedience.

To say that absolutely everyone has been infected by Adam, but you must make a decision to be affected by Christ, renders the Gospel as little more than a joke.

However, according to the common usage of the Greek word in Greek literature, the word carries within it an absolute definitive outcome—ALL (everyone) will be saved and come to the knowledge of the truth.

It is impossible to consider that the word "all" only refers to "some" in most of these passages concerning our salvation.

Verdict: Fiction

ALL usually means everyone, especially when used in the context of our salvation.

13
OBJECTION—
WARN THE WICKED

Fact or Fiction

Universalism does away with warning the wicked

I had never considered this objection until it was presented to me as a response to my survey.

> **Objection:** Then you will undoubtedly need to go back and read Ezekiel 3:17-21. God made us watchmen, tasking us to warn those in error of that error. If they repent, then God is happy. If they don't, then it's on them alone.
>
> But if we don't warn, 'then they will die in their sin, and [emphasis added] I WILL HOLD YOU RESPONSIBLE FOR THEIR BLOOD.' Pretty clear to me.

This objection arises from the assumption that belief in the all-encompassing love of God for His creation renders unnecessary the call to warn the wicked.

Before addressing all that is problematic with this objection as presented, I will say this: the assumption is correct. Warning the wicked—as a means of saving them from hell—is not on the radar of most universalists. Most Universalists take the Bible in a more literal fashion than our brothers and sisters of Arminian or Reformed persuasion (as you have hopefully seen throughout this book).

The first point to address is the closing remark in the objection: "Pretty clear to me." Any casual observation of Bible believers should reveal that what is plain to one person is not necessarily plain to another—and certainly not to all.

> We often make such statements as though they were a trump card meant to settle the matter.

It may indeed be clear to you, but that does not make it universally clear. A better and more compassionate way to express the same conviction might be, "The way I understand this passage is…"

Let us each try to adopt the language of love and acceptance when engaging one another—especially when discussing what we believe the Bible says.

We had a joke going around when I was in Bible college. Our Systematic Theology class used a book by R. A. Torrey entitled *What the Bible Teaches*. We would say to each other, "What the Bible teaches Torrey." Little did we know how right we were in those days.

The second consideration of this objection is the location of the passage itself. It comes from the prophet Ezekiel, who was commissioned to prophesy to the house of Israel. These statements must first be considered in their original context and intent.

There is nothing in this passage to indicate that these words were meant for anyone other than Israel.

We must once again consider what I emphasized in Chapter Three about how to read the Bible. Are we required to take every word of Scripture and make it directly applicable to ourselves? Obviously not, because we are not called to prophesy to the house of Israel.

Are we supposed to go to a high priest and present an animal offering for sacrifice? No.

No rule requires us to engage in such foolishness.

Taking this passage and applying it indiscriminately to believers has no biblical basis. We have bought into the rules, regulations, and traditions of men, which render the word of God ineffectual (Mark 7:7-8).

We have also allowed our understanding of the inspiration of Scripture to carry us far beyond what the original statement on inspiration (2 Timothy 3:16) intended.

Thirdly—following directly from the previous point—we must ask whether this is *really* our responsibility.

Are each of us appointed as watchmen to "warn the wicked"?

Perhaps it is this misapplied passage that has resulted in so many of "God's policemen" being loosed upon the Body of Christ. There are far too many unqualified individuals attempting to warn others about their "sin."

This is *not* the teaching found in the New Testament.

> "Brothers, if anyone is caught in any
> transgression, you who are spiritual
> should restore him in a spirit of
> gentleness. Keep watch on yourself,
> lest you too be tempted" (Galatians
> 6:1).

Notice that it is the *spiritual* ones who are to address someone caught in a fault.

I am not going to unpack that verse here, but it should be noted that not *all* are spiritual, not by any stretch of the imagination. This fact alone renders the universal application of Ezekiel's warning passage to every believer an exercise in futility.

Not only that, but Jesus Himself issued a strong condemnation of this attitude:

> "How can you say to your brother, 'Brother, let me take out the speck that is in your eye,' when you yourself do not see the log that is in your own eye? You hypocrite, first take the log out of your own eye, and then you will see clearly to take out the speck that is in your brother's eye" (Luke 6:42).

The problem is that people take this passage and apply it to themselves without any understanding of what it means to "warn the wicked."

What is *your* concept of wickedness?
Is it the same as everyone else's concept?
What makes your understanding the correct one?
What makes you so special?

Consider this—there was a time when it was considered "wicked" for a woman's ankles to be visible. There was a time when it was immoral for a woman to be seen smoking a cigarette in public. There was a time when it was regarded as unholy for a man to wear short-sleeved shirts. There was also a time when it was considered inappropriate for a man to go out in public without a hat.

All of these improprieties have fallen by the wayside, but there was a time when "God's policemen" would call you to task for violating one of these so-called rules.

You may want to argue with me and say, "Yes, but this is about *true* wickedness—things like murder, drunkenness, and adultery. We are to warn people not to do such things."

Really?

Perhaps you should warn Jesus about that.

He failed to warn the woman at the well or the woman caught in adultery.

For the sake of argument, I will allow "Go and sin no more" as a possible "warning," but it was not. Nor was it a command. (I AM NOT GOING TO ADDRESS THAT MISINTERPRETATION AT THIS TIME, SO THAT I MAY STAY ON POINT.)

The issue, then, becomes this: what is the wickedness of which we are supposed to warn people?

Reading the passage referred to in Ezekiel 3:17ff., we find that nothing is plainly stated. The closest we get is this: *"If I say to the wicked, 'You shall die...'"* That is it. Nothing further is brought to light. It is simply a warning about a possible death that is about to occur.

When we read the entire passage—from verses 17 through 21—we see that the warning carries consequences for both failing to warn and failing to heed the warning: death.

Those who use this passage to argue against the concept of universal salvation assume that the "death" spoken of here refers to being eternally locked away in hell.

I cannot find that interpretation in any translation of this passage.

"Dying in your sins" simply means that one has died without the issue of sin being resolved. And if I failed to warn you, then your blood is on me.

Blood has no bearing on the afterlife. It pertains only to life on this plane of existence. Jesus said,

> "See my hands and my feet, that it is I myself.
> Touch me and see. For a spirit does not
> have flesh and bones as you see that I
> have" (Luke 24:39).

He said nothing about blood after the resurrection, because it had all been "poured out" for a purpose before He died.

To take the concept of dying as presented in this passage and make it refer to spending an eternity in hell has no basis except in the imagination.

What, then, about the final part of the objection: "I WILL HOLD YOU RESPONSIBLE FOR THEIR BLOOD"?

An extremely important point is missed when this guilt is laid upon others. Who says that *we* have been made watchmen? Is that truly our responsibility?

Listen to the apostle Paul: "Who are you to pass judgment on the servant of another? It is before his own master that he stands or falls. And he will be upheld, for the Lord is able to make him stand" (Romans 14:4).

When Jesus gave the Sermon on the Mount, He continually quoted something His listeners were familiar with and followed it with, "… but I say to you."

He was turning the old order on its ear.
He was not trying to enhance it or make it more palatable.

He then addressed the result of legalism—judgmentalism—and told them not to participate in it.

> "Judge not, that you be not judged. For with the judgment you pronounce you will be judged, and with the measure you use it will be measured to you" (Matthew 7:1-2).

The second verse should give all hell-believers pause. When you tell someone they are going to hell, you have judged them. According to Jesus, you have just pronounced the same judgment upon yourself.

Later in His ministry, Jesus speaks even more directly about His own role regarding judgment: "You judge according to the flesh; I judge no one" (John 8:15).

Since the author and finisher of our faith (Hebrews 12:2) does not judge or condemn anyone, why do we think that we should?

Is He not our example?

The closest example we have of Jesus judging anyone is when He rebuked the Pharisees, scribes, and Sadducees. They were the ones who judged everyone else for their inability to keep the minutiae of the law. They were the ones who enforced legalistic standards for pleasing God. Those who today claim that we should warn others of their wickedness are the descendants of these same religious hypocrites.

Even though we believe we should follow what Jesus taught, we still do not have the authority to judge those who either do not believe as we do or are not able to follow His teachings.

> "If anyone hears my words and does not keep
> them, I do not judge him; for I did not
> come to judge the world but to save the
> world" (John 12:47).

Attempting to use an Old Testament passage to justify confronting people about their sin completely nullifies what both Jesus and Paul teach us in the New Testament. Therefore, choose this day whom you will follow. If Moses is lord, then follow him; but if Jesus is Lord, then follow Him.

Verdict: Fiction

It is the New Testament that does away with warning the wicked.

14
JOHN 3:16

Fact or Fiction

John 3:16 proves that we must accept Jesus in order to be saved

Probably the most well-known verse in the entire Bible is John 3:16:

> "For God so loved the world, that he gave his
> only Son, that whoever believes in him
> should not perish but have eternal life."

You can see it on signs along the back roads of our country, posted on billboards near cities, or referenced at almost every football game by someone sitting in the end-zone seats. I would venture to say that most non-believers have some idea of what the verse says, even if they can't quote it.

Whenever I refer to this verse, I like to ask, "What condition was the world in when Jesus came? Was it good? Was it lovable? Obviously not."

God loved the world in the condition it was in at the time.

There was political corruption, oppression of the poor, religious leaders lining their pockets, open prostitution, thievery, and all the other ills that still plague society today.

That is the world God loved so much that He sent Jesus into it.

God did not wait for people to return to the synagogue or get their act together. He loved, and He gave. All of this still holds true today.

God is not waiting for you to clean up your life before He will accept you.

Yet this is not what so many people have indirectly been taught through our misinformed ministries. Invite someone to church, and they will often respond with something like, "I'm not ready to give up… (whatever)."

Where did they get the idea that they had to quit whatever it is in order to come to church? The same holds true for trying to "bring them to Jesus." They feel they cannot be accepted by the Lord until they are able to behave better.

God sent the Son long before anyone was able to be good. No one was righteous or good—not even one (SEE PSALM 14:3; 53:3; ROMANS 3:10).

Therefore, the first thing to understand is that God knew our sinful condition and that we couldn't do anything about it on our own. We needed help. That help came in the person of Jesus Christ.

Most Christians believe, accept, and agree on this part of the verse.

It is the next part of the verse, though, that seems to give us trouble —"…*whoever believes in him.*"

What are we to make of this?

Essentially, we have made *belief* the touchstone of salvation. If a person does not believe, they cannot be saved. While that may be true, it is not necessarily the precursor to salvation.

Is it not possible that belief is simply an indicator of an existing reality? Those who are saved believe. Those who believe are the ones who have eternal life.

This may be a finer line than some are comfortable drawing, but the point remains: belief, in and of itself, does not produce salvation.

However, since we have made belief a prerequisite to salvation, we run into other problems within the differing schools of thought.

Arminians, with their focus on the free will of man, use this verse to "prove" that man has free will—even though that concept is not stated here. They argue that since it is up to us to believe, this proves free will. And it should be obvious that not everyone chooses to believe.

Calvinists, on the other hand, with their focus on God's election, maintain that only the elect can believe, and because of irresistible grace, they will believe. Yet they, too, place belief as the required first step for salvation to be realized.

Both schools ultimately require human effort: the ability to recognize the "logic" of God's plan and choose, by one means or another, to accept the offer.

I choose, however, to go with what Scripture says about our faith to believe:

> "For by grace you have been saved through
>   faith. And this is not your own doing; it is
>   the gift of God" (Ephesians 2:8, ESV)

If you can read this verse without filters, consider what "the gift of God" refers to.

Is it grace?
Grace is certainly a gift.

Is it salvation?
Salvation is also a gift.

But what about faith?
Can faith itself be a gift?

This is where we often get hung up. We have been taught that faith is something we do. We believe. We activate our "believer mechanism" so that we can "believe God" for something.

But is that what the Bible teaches about faith for salvation?

Consider Paul's statement in his letter to the Galatians:

> "I am crucified with Christ: nevertheless I
>   live; yet not I, but Christ lives in me: and
>   the life which I now live in the flesh I live
>   by the **faith of the Son of God**, who
>   loved me, and gave himself for me."
>   (Galatians 2:20, KJV; emphasis added)

The phrase "faith of the Son of God" is the important point for us to consider.

Most modern translations render this phrase as "faith in the Son of God." Older translations—such as the King James, Darby, Webster, Young's Literal, and others—retain "of" rather than "in": "faith of the Son of God."

It is important to note that translations, regardless of their origin, are interpretive. Whoever produced the translation brought a particular bias, perspective, or theological framework to the task, and that bias inevitably affects the translation. This is not to suggest that such bias is necessarily wrong or harmful.

Here is the key point: there is no preposition in the original Greek corresponding to either "in" or "of" within the phrase "faith of the Son of God." The appearance of a preposition in English arises from how the relationship between the nouns is rendered.

> The Greek word construction in this verse places "Son of God" in the genitive case (a grammatical form that does not map cleanly onto English). The genitive case expresses relationships between nouns and is commonly translated using the English words "of" or "from.[1]

The modern translations have taken their cue from the common thought of the day, which is that we must exercise our faith and place it in Jesus. However, the Greek construction of the phrase leaves us with only adding "of" or "from."

In this case, therefore, we have the faith which is "of Jesus," or "from Jesus." It is His faith, not ours.

Therefore, considering our verse in its entirety, we can answer the question posed from Ephesians 2:8. Faith is also the gift of God.

It is God who gives us the faith to believe.
It is God who gives us the gift of salvation.
It is God who gives us the gift of grace.

And the life we now live in the flesh, we live because of the faith of the Son of God, Jesus.

It is His faith that sustains me—not mine. My faith is weak.

It is not necessary for me to summon all my strength and press through, trying to believe God. He has given me the faith to believe.

Please allow me to tell a little story here.

I never walked the aisle to the altar to confess my sins and accept Jesus as my personal savior. In my early years with the Lord, because

---

1. John William White, *First Greek Book: A Digital Tutorial for Ancient Greek.*

I associated with those who believed that act was the necessary process for salvation, I often had doubts about my salvation.

There were many times when I would be reduced to tears, crying out to the Lord to make my salvation real to me. This was my process for almost forty-five years.

Then, one day, while I was driving and thinking, I once again began to struggle. "Lord, it is so easy for some, but it's not for me. I have doubts. I see how easy it would be just to cast this whole thing aside, because so much of it defies logic. But I believe, Lord. I believe."

In that moment, I felt a warmth flow over my body as the tears began to fall. I knew then that I belonged to Him. There has not been a doubt since.

I have even expressed the thought, "Maybe that was when I really got saved." However, I know that is not true, which is something I will explain later on.

John 3:16 is certainly a key verse in the Bible, but it needs to be understood in the light of the rest of Scripture—not simply from man's interpretation of this single verse.

For now, as applied to John 3:16, we must admit that the idea of choice is not the main thought of this verse. Not only is it not the main thought, but it is also not even implied.

Believing in Jesus is a simple statement of fact in this verse.

Verdict: Fiction

John 3:16 is a statement of fact.

15
OBJECTIONS SUMMARIZED

Fact or Fiction

Universalists ignore verses which prove them wrong

I am always encouraged by people discussing the taboo topics of Christianity. When people are discussing and debating issues like hell, the rapture, and different types of atonement, it is a good sign that fear is no longer their primary motivator and that they are finally using their minds to evaluate what they believe. That is extremely healthy.

Anyone who is honest knows that it is impossible to disprove Universalism from Scripture, because Scripture can be used to support or reject just about anything.

An honest person will say that they disagree with the position of Universalism, but ultimately, it is nothing more than special pleading. That is, they choose to interpret the verses that support their position as clearer and superior to the verses that support Universalism. There is nothing wrong with a person choosing to do that, as long as they are honest about it.

The problem arises when they then try to use loaded questions, flawed logic, and outright lies about Scripture to guilt and shame people into their position. Unfortunately, all too often, the people who try to make these arguments have no idea what Universalism is or have never taken the time to read any Universalist works to understand the arguments.

That brings me to the first point. Universalism is not the same thing as not believing in hell.

So when a person starts to point out all the supposed hell passages as some sort of evidence against Universalism, that person does not know what they are talking about.

Many streams of Christian Universalism believe in hell, but not as a form of eternal punishment and torture. Instead, it is viewed as a place of temporary refinement and restoration.

When a person claims that it is only through Christ that we must be saved as some sort of rebuff against Universalism, again, that person does not know what Universalists believe.

All strands of Christian Universalism believe that it is through Christ that people shall be saved. They simply disagree with the idea that this can only happen in this life, based on a choice or decision made within the few short years allotted to us.

One friend, adamantly opposed to the teaching that God intends to save everyone, would regularly tell me I was ignoring the objections she raised. The problem was that she would send me at least eight "what about…" objections in each missive. Attached to each was a long, rambling string of mostly incoherent thoughts.

When I would try to get her to focus on just one for discussion, she would become angry.

She also claimed that Universalism is a new doctrine built upon redefining words to suit the teaching.

When I asked whether she had read my first book, she replied that there was no need to do so, because she already understood the teaching of Universalism perfectly.

To say that Universalism is a "new doctrine" ignores the history of the doctrine, which is available to anyone who is willing to search.

To say that it is "built upon redefining words to suit the teaching" also ignores the history of language itself.

All languages go through changes in idiom, syntax, and vocabulary. While it may be argued that current meanings are the ones we should use, doing so would ignore the intent of the ancient authors.

Therefore, yes, we do "redefine" words—by returning them to their original intent.

However, we are not making up our own definitions to suit the teaching.

We derive the teaching from the original meanings of the words used by the authors themselves. We gain insight into those meanings from scholars—those accepted across all streams of biblical studies —who provide cultural and linguistic context for the times in which the texts were written.

> By "accepted scholars," I mean works such as *Vine's Expository Dictionary*, *Thayer's Greek Lexicon*, *Kittel's Theological Dictionary of New Testament Words*, *Brown, Driver, and Briggs Hebrew Lexicon*, and others. These are standard reference works that any Bible student can access, regardless of their level of language education.

When I read most objections people raise, I find that the majority arise from attempts to reason "logically" and conclude that if one thing is true, then something else cannot be true.

I have yet to encounter someone who reasons this way who has also taken the time to seriously examine the teaching.

Instead, assumptions are made based on sound bites that have been heard, without any in-depth investigation into why those sound bites exist.

A good example of this was discussed in Chapter 6. The seemingly "logical" conclusion is that if Universalism is true, then there is no need to evangelize, since everyone will be saved in the end.

This line of reasoning reveals both a misunderstanding of evangelism and a misunderstanding of Universalism.

The same could be said of nearly every "logical" objection that is raised.

However, there are some objections that are rooted in specific verses or passages of Scripture. I have far more respect for these than for the others.

One of my purposes in writing this book is to present a biblical look into the teaching known (among other things) as Universalism.

In order to present a truly biblical study, it is necessary that I also include those verses that seem to contradict any idea of the inclusion of the entire human race in God's plan of salvation.

I am not aware of every single verse that could be used against this teaching, but I believe what I present in this chapter will suffice to show that opposing verses, when properly understood, do not pose a problem for the grace, mercy, and love of God.

There may indeed be one or more verses that I cannot answer from my viewpoint, but I believe the overwhelming majority of so-called "gotcha verses" are easily explained in the light of God's love.

We have already considered the concept of judgment in Chapter 10, but I have not yet examined the idea of "perish."

This is another word that gives people difficulty when considering the belief that God will restore all things to their original condition (Acts 3:21).

The word "perish" appears 108 times in the ESV and 120 times in the KJV. It is used ninety times in the Old Testament (ESV) and eighteen times in the New Testament (ESV).

There are 10 different Hebrew words translated as *perish* in the Old Testament, and 7 different Greek words in the New Testament. In most cases, one word dominates usage, while many of the others appear only once.

The two primary words are the Hebrew *ābad* (Strong's H6), which appears 184 times in various forms, and the Greek *apollymi* (Strong's G622), which appears 92 times in various forms.

Those who hold to the doctrine of eternal conscious torment (ECT) interpret most verses containing the word "perish" as referring to hell for all eternity.

There are some verses that could be construed this way—but only if one is already approaching the text from the perspective of ECT.

When these verses are read without that filter, it becomes clear that "perish" almost always refers to the cessation of life on this plane of existence.

For example:

> By faith, Rahab the prostitute did not perish
> with those who were disobedient, because
> she had given a friendly welcome to the
> spies. (Hebrews 11:31)

This clearly refers to physical death. In fact, this is the case in 12 of the 18 New Testament occurrences of the word in the ESV.

Given this, why do we assume the minority usage represents the primary theological meaning?

There are a few instances in which the word could be interpreted either physically or spiritually, such as:

> "For God so loved the world, that he gave his
> only Son, that whoever believes in him
> should not perish but have eternal life."
> (John 3:16)

This verse, of course, serves as a foundational text for many Christians in establishing a contrast between heaven and hell. If taken literally as referring to physical death, it implies immortality within this present realm. If taken spiritually, it suggests annihilation of the soul.

To be honest, I do not take a firm position on the meaning of "perish" in this verse, as my focus rests primarily on the promise of eternal life. Eternal life speaks more to quality than to quantity.

I am still waiting for the Lord to unveil for me the meaning of "perish" in this verse and in the few others like it. However, it is nearly impossible to read this passage as a statement about hell without engaging in significant mental gymnastics.

SIN IN THE PRESENCE OF GOD

Another major objection to the idea that everyone will be saved is the claim that God cannot look upon or accept sin. The primary basis for this idea is found in the prophet Habakkuk:

> You who are of purer eyes than to see evil
> and cannot look at wrong,
> why do you idly look at traitors
> and remain silent when the wicked
> swallows up
> the man more righteous than he?
> (Habakkuk 1:13)

The "proof" often offered for this interpretation is Jesus' cry from the cross:

> "And about the ninth hour, Jesus cried out
>   with a loud voice, saying, 'Eli, Eli, lema
>   sabachthani?' that is, 'My God, my God,
>   why have you forsaken me?'" (Matthew
>   27:46)

However, using a literal, historical-grammatical approach to interpretation, we find a very different understanding. (Literal, historical-grammatical interpretation is the hermeneutic espoused by most evangelical scholars and preachers—whether universalist or not.)

When Jesus cried out in anguish, was He stating a doctrinal fact? Should we conclude from His cry that God had actually abandoned Him?

Sadly, this is what is taught in many pulpits today, but it ignores the broader witness of Scripture—something Universalists are often accused of doing.

One verse frequently quoted as encouragement for the downtrodden states:

> "Keep your life free from love of money, and
>   be content with what you have, for he has
>   said, 'I will never leave you nor forsake
>   you.'" (Hebrews 13:5)

The promise "I will not leave you" appears numerous times in the Old Testament—sometimes spoken to individuals, sometimes as a general assurance.

So the question remains: did God forsake Jesus? Could He?

Of course not.

What, then, are we to make of Jesus' cry?

It is unfortunate that this even needs explanation, but given the distorted teaching that exists today, it is necessary.

Jesus was tempted in all things just as we are, yet without sin (Hebrews 4:15). Have you never felt abandoned by God? Have you never experienced a season when the heavens felt like brass, and your prayers seemed to go no higher than the ceiling?

It is easy to see that this is precisely what Jesus was experiencing in His humanity. This is not evidence that God abandoned Him because He could not look upon sin.

We must also reconsider the verse from Habakkuk itself:

> "You who are of purer eyes than to see evil
>   and cannot look at wrong…" (Hab. 1:13)

To use this statement as a doctrinal assertion about God violates basic rules of interpretation:

Who said this?
A man.
Why did he say it?
He was lamenting the conditions of his time (Habakkuk 1:1–4).

This verse about God's eyes of purity follows God's declaration that He was raising up the Chaldeans to punish Israel. Everything Habakkuk repeats as an oracle from God concerns the evil actions of the Chaldeans.

If God cannot look upon evil, how then does He declare that He is raising up *"a bitter and hasty nation… whose own might is their god"*?

The answer is simple: we have taken a human complaint spoken in anguish and elevated it into a doctrinal statement about God's nature.

How often does this happen? After a tragedy, people frequently ask, "Why did God allow this to happen?" Do we accept that question as a theological declaration about God's control over all events?

The same mistake is being made here with Habakkuk.

DESTRUCTION

> They will suffer the punishment of eternal
> destruction, from the presence of the
> Lord and from the glory of his might
> (2 Thessalonians 1:9).

From translates the Greek word *apo*, which, as used in Scripture and in literature written before Christ, carries a range of meanings—as is true of most prepositions.

For instance, consider Thayer's Greek Lexicon as found in the Blue Letter Bible app: *"of the efficient cause, viz. of things from the force of which anything proceeds, and of persons from whose will, power, authority, command, favor, order, influence, direction, anything is to be sought."*

Thayer cites this passage as one of the many instances illustrating this usage. The word *away* is an interpretive addition supplied by the translators.

What we would thus understand, then, is that the age-during justice comes *from* the Lord, not that it consists of being kept *away from* His presence. This is a completely different meaning than the one commonly assumed. Therefore, this passage fits consistently with the premise of God's plan to save all.

What is described as "punishment" is not punitive in nature, but corrective or remedial in nature.

The concept of "everlasting" has been addressed numerous times already, so I will not belabor that point here.

What I *do* find fascinating, however, is the word translated as *destruction*. It is not the word *apollumi*, as one might expect. Instead, it is a term used only 4 times in the New Testament. In the other 3 occurrences, the word refers to the destruction of the flesh.

Therefore, to take this verse and make it signify something entirely different is out of line with normal biblical interpretation.

Once again, this verse aligns with what I see throughout Scripture regarding God's plan for humanity.

Verdict: Fiction

Universalists are generally willing to explain how any verse fits within God's plan to save everyone

AFTERWORD

Regardless of which side one falls on—for or against the belief that God loves His entire creation—it should be acknowledged that there are clear passages which proclaim His unending love for all and His intention to save all. It is equally true that there are verses that seem to teach otherwise.

Neither side should be willing to concede that the Bible contradicts itself. However, we **must** recognize that our underlying paradigm determines how we understand the overall teaching of Scripture.

If we begin with the paradigm of God's love, we can see how it is quite possible that the verses teaching the eventual salvation of all are the majority view. If we begin with the paradigm of God's justice, then we are left with the idea that God grants humanity only a brief window—approximately seventy years—to make an eternal decision.

The primary objection to God's unending mercy is the concept of judgment and punishment for evil. When passages concerning judgment and God's justice (see Chapters 10 and 11) are filtered through a preconceived doctrine of eternal conscious torment for unbelievers, the objection appears compelling. However, when those same passages are read within their proper context, it becomes evident that we have imported our own desire for punishment into them. Nearly every passage addressing judgment refers to something that takes place in this life.

Yes, there may be a small number of verses that seem to point toward something unending—but does an exception invalidate the rule? Why should one or two passages be allowed to define our entire understanding of God's justice, while the many verses in both the Old and New Testaments declaring that our guilt for sin was removed and nailed to the cross of Jesus Christ are overlooked?

Can I answer every objection to the concept known as Universalism? No. Nor do I need to. I also do not need to deny what I have come to see clearly after many years of standing firmly on the other side.

Will I go to hell for my belief? Of course not, for *"everyone who calls on the name of the Lord shall be saved"* (Romans 10:13). Will I go to hell because my belief might lead others astray? Again, no. Like those who believe in an eternal hell, I tell people, "God loves you and has a wonderful plan for your life." Will I go to hell because my belief supposedly gives people a "license to sin"? Certainly not. Everyone already possesses their own license to sin—whether they believe in God and His love or not.

I did not begin following the Lord out of fear of hell. I began following Him because I recognized the value and benefits of doing so. Those benefits are experienced in this life in ways that make my experience impossible to deny.

I would rather err on the side of love than on the side of fear. The foundational verse for most Christians is John 3:16, which begins by emphasizing God's love—*"For God so loved the world..."*

Consider this: from a purely human and logical standpoint, do people obey the law only when police are visible? Many do. When enforcement disappears, behavior often changes. That kind of obedience is not motivated by love but by fear of punishment. John tells us this is not how we are meant to live (1 John 4:18).

I maintain that if people must be frightened into the kingdom, then fear must also be used to keep them there. Even then, fear alone cannot sustain obedience indefinitely.

If you have taken the time to read this entire book, I hope something within it caused you to pause and reflect. Whether or not you agree with my conclusions, I trust you now understand the biblical foundation for the universalist position. While historical and logical arguments also exist, this book has focused on Scripture as the primary foundation.

If you gained anything from reading this book—whether a strengthened confidence in love or a deeper appreciation for justice —I would welcome your feedback. You may email me at dalehill47@gmail.com with *"I READ YOUR BOOK"* in the subject line. Thank you.

You can also find more content on my YouTube channel at https://www.youtube.com/@dalehill47 or by searching Practical Bible Teaching.

APPENDIX 1
A COMPENDIUM
OF MAJOR PROOFS

The purpose of this book is to provide the reader with biblical proofs for the salvation of all.

Some readers need this material for themselves, while others need it to help answer questions from friends. Still others may wish to give this book to friends who are asking questions.

This appendix brings together many of the verses discussed in earlier chapters, along with some that were not.

Its purpose is to give the reader quick and easy access to the major passages supporting God's love and mercy toward all humanity.

The verses included here are not discussed in depth—some not at all. Many are presented without full context, but it is assumed that a serious student will consider the surrounding context of each passage.

You may find that although some verses are technically "out of context," they are not, therefore, outside the truth.

Some Key Verses

Romans 5:18–19

Therefore, as one trespass led to condemnation for all men, so one act of righteousness leads to justification and life for all men. For as by the one man's disobedience the many were made sinners, so by the one man's obedience the many will be made righteous.

Remark:

The central argument of Romans 5:12-21 is that ALL came under condemnation through Adam and that ALL are made righteous through Christ. The "many" in verse 19 functions as a synonym for "all." Grace triumphs over sin.

What Christ accomplished surpasses what Adam did. To claim that Adam condemned all, but Christ saves only a few, contradicts the entire thrust of the passage.

Verse 19 often causes confusion because readers focus on "the many" who are made righteous while overlooking that the exact same phrase—*the many*—is also used of those made sinners through Adam.

We readily accept that "the many" made sinners refers to everyone. Why, then, do we shift meanings in the next reference?

1 Corinthians 15:21–22

For as by a man came death, by a man has come also the resurrection of the dead. For as in Adam all die, so also in Christ shall all be made alive.

Remark:

It is misleading to claim that the "all" in Adam differs from the "all" in Christ. Paul's theology consistently presents Christ as reversing the effects of Adam. This theme is central to his arguments in both Romans and Corinthians.

The claim that "not everyone is in Christ" imports an assumption into the text. Paul states the matter plainly: everyone shall be made alive in Christ. The timing is not his concern.

1 Timothy 2:3–6

This is good, and it is pleasing in the sight of God our Savior, who desires all people to be saved and to come to the knowledge of the truth. For there is one God, and there is one mediator between God and men, the man Christ Jesus, who gave himself as a ransom for all, which is the testimony given at the proper time.

Remark:

God's will is that everyone will be saved. Ultimately, God's will shall be accomplished. He wants to save everyone, and he will—or He is not God.

If Jesus "gave Himself as a ransom for all," is it not a cruel joke to think that some will not be ransomed?

2 Corinthians 5:19

That is, in Christ God was reconciling the world to himself, not counting their trespasses against them, and entrusting to us the message of reconciliation.

Remark:

The Greek word translated as "world" literally means "cosmos." God reconciled the whole cosmos to himself. Cosmos refers to the entire physical creation.

Notice that in this reconciliation process, God was "not counting their trespasses against them." Yet many emphasize the necessity to repent before one can claim to be saved.

Colossians 1:19-20

For in him all the fullness of God was pleased to dwell, and through him to reconcile to himself all things, whether on earth or in heaven, making peace by the blood of his cross.

Remark:

These verses are part of the creed of faith of the very first believers. It shows that they understood the work of Christ in universal terms. All things have been reconciled. ALL THINGS—whether in heaven or on earth.

Romans 11:32

For God has consigned all to disobedience, that he may have mercy on all.

Remark:

Paul concludes his whole argument from Romans chapters one through eleven with this verse! God will show mercy to all. That's the central message of Paul's letter to the Romans. God's mercy will triumph over man's disobedience.

Acts 3:21

whom heaven must receive until the time for restoring all the things about which God spoke by the mouth of his holy prophets long ago.

Matthew 18:11 (KJV)

For the Son of man is come to save that which was lost.

Remark:

Jesus plainly stated His purpose to be that of saving the lost.

Are we to believe that He is so impotent as to have failed in that mission?

That He is only able to save SOME of the lost?

Matthew 26:27-28

And he took a cup, and when he had given thanks, he gave it to them, saying, "Drink of it, all of you, for this is my blood of the covenant, which is poured out for many for the forgiveness of sins."

Remark:

The adjective *many* is not restrictive in the sense of excluding some; rather, it is all-inclusive, as it frequently is in the Hebrew of the Old Testament, and many translations have "all people."

John—in his gospel and in his letters—constantly portrayed Jesus as the Savior of the whole world.

John 1:29

The next day, he saw Jesus coming toward him and said, "Behold, the Lamb of God, who takes away the sin of the world!"

John 4:42

They said to the woman, "It is no longer because of what you said that we believe, for we have heard for ourselves, and we know that this is indeed the Savior of the world."

John 12:32

And I, when I am lifted up from the earth, will draw all people to myself.

Remark:

Many interpreters claim that "all people" actually means people from all nations. Why didn't Jesus say it that way if that was what He meant?

John 12:47

If anyone hears my words and does not keep them, I do not judge him; for I did not come to judge the world but to save the world.

1 John 2:1-2

My little children, I am writing these things to you so that you may not sin. But if anyone does sin, we have an advocate with the Father, Jesus Christ the righteous. He is the propitiation for our sins, and not for ours only, but also for the sins of the whole world.

Remark:

Many believe and teach that Jesus is not our Savior until we accept Him. However, He is the propitiation for the believer's sins and for the sins of the whole world.

1 John 4:14

And we have seen and testify that the Father has sent his Son to be the Savior of the world.

More New Testament verses that point toward a universal reconciliation:

1 Timothy 4:10

For to this end we toil and strive, because we have our hope set on the living God, who is the Savior of all people, especially of those who believe.

Phil 2: 10-11

so that at the name of Jesus every knee should bow, in heaven and on earth and under the earth, and every tongue confess that Jesus Christ is Lord, to the glory of God the Father.

Remark:

We know that this confession will not be forced but will come from a sincere heart, because only the Holy Spirit can bring it forth (SEE 1 CORINTHIANS 12:3).

Ephesians 1:9-10

making known to us the mystery of his will, according to his purpose, which he set forth in Christ as a plan for the fullness of time, to unite all things in him, things in heaven and things on earth.

2 Peter 3:9

The Lord is not slow to fulfill his promise as some count slowness, but is patient toward you, not wishing that any should perish, but that all should reach repentance.

Titus 2:11

For the grace of God has appeared, bringing salvation for all people.

Ephesians 4:10

He who descended is the one who also ascended far above all the heavens, that he might fill all things.

Matthew 25:46 (YLT)

And these shall go away to punishment age-during, but the righteous to life age-during.

Remark:

Read more about this parable and its meaning HERE.[1]

Matthew 13:33

He told them another parable. "The kingdom of heaven is like leaven that a woman took and hid in three measures of flour, till it was all leavened."

Matthew 18:34-35 (NET)

And in anger, his lord turned him over to the prison guards to torture him until he repaid all he owed. So also my heavenly Father will do to you, if each of you does not forgive your brother from your heart.

Remark:

This verse is often used to prove that not everyone is saved, because this verse shows that the wicked are turned over for torture. However, what is usually missed is that there is a time limit to the imprisonment.

Luke 19:10

For the Son of Man came to seek and to save the lost.

---

1. (https://www.jesusreformation.org/en/2021/does-the-parable-of-the-sheep-and-the-goats-teach-hell-or-universal-reconciliation/)

Revelation 21:25-22:2 (NET)

Its gates will never be closed during the day (and there will be no night there). They will bring the grandeur and the wealth of the nations into it, but nothing ritually unclean will ever enter into it, nor anyone who does what is detestable or practices falsehood, but only those whose names are written in the Lamb's book of life. Then the angel showed me the river of the water of life—water as clear as crystal—pouring out from the throne of God and of the Lamb, flowing down the middle of the city's main street. On each side of the river is the tree of life producing twelve kinds of fruit, yielding its fruit every month of the year. Its leaves are for the healing of the nations.

Remark:

Outside of New Jerusalem are the ones that didn't repent yet (Revelation 22:15), those who were thrown into the lake of fire (according to Revelation 21:1-8).

The gates of New Jerusalem will never be shut. God's mercy will never come to an end. The leaves in the city are for the healing of the nations.

Revelation ends with God's invitation: *"And the Spirit and the bride say, 'Come!' And let the one who hears say: 'Come!' And let the one who is thirsty come; let the one who wants it take the water of life free of charge"* (Revelation 22:17 NET).

God's loyal love endures forever. The Father always waits with open arms, just as Jesus taught us (Luke 15:20).

Hebrews 2:9

But we see him who for a little while was made lower than the angels, namely Jesus, crowned with glory and honor because of the suffering of death, so that by the grace of God he might taste death for everyone.

Hebrews 8:11-12

"And they shall not teach, each one his neighbor and each one his brother, saying, 'Know the Lord,' for they shall all know me, from the least of them to the greatest. For I will be merciful toward their iniquities, and I will remember their sins no more."

James 2:13

For judgment is without mercy to one who has shown no mercy. Mercy triumphs over judgment.

Romans 11:32

For God has consigned all to disobedience, that he may have mercy on all.

Verses from the Old Testament:

1 Chronicles 16:34 (NET)

Give thanks to the Lord, for he is good and his loyal love endures.

Remark:

The phrase "God's loyal love will endure (forever)" is the most repeated description of God in the Old Testament! God's loyal love will never come to an end. This is certain.

Lamentations 3:22-23

The steadfast love of the LORD never ceases; his mercies never come to an end; they are new every morning; great is your faithfulness.

Isaiah 25:6-8

On this mountain, the LORD of hosts will make for all peoples a feast of rich food, a feast of well-aged wine, of rich food full of marrow, of aged wine well refined. And he will swallow up on this mountain the covering that is cast over all peoples, the veil that is spread over all nations. He will swallow up death forever; and the Lord GOD will wipe away tears from all faces, and the reproach of his people he will take away from all the earth, for the LORD has spoken.

Psalm 30:5

For his anger is but for a moment, and his favor is for a lifetime. Weeping may tarry for the night, but joy comes with the morning.

Psalm 103:8-10

The LORD is merciful and gracious, slow to anger and abounding in steadfast love. He will not always chide, nor will he keep his anger forever. He does not deal with us according to our sins, nor repay us according to our iniquities.

Isaiah 53:6

All we like sheep have gone astray; we have turned—everyone—to his own way; and the LORD has laid on him the iniquity of us all.

Psalm 145:8-9

The LORD is gracious and merciful, slow to anger and abounding in steadfast love. The LORD is good to all, and his mercy is over all that he has made.

Psalm 22:27-29

All the ends of the earth shall remember and turn to the LORD, and all the families of the nations shall worship before you. For kingship belongs to the LORD, and he rules over the nations. All the prosperous of the earth eat and worship; before him shall bow all who go down to the dust, even the one who could not keep himself alive.

Psalm 65:3

When iniquities prevail against me, you atone for our transgressions.

Lamentation 3:31-33

For the Lord will not cast off forever, but, though he cause grief, he will have compassion according to the abundance of his steadfast love; for he does not afflict from his heart or grieve the children of men.

Isaiah 57:16

For I will not contend forever, nor will I always be angry; for the spirit would grow faint before me, and the breath of life that I made.

2 Samuel 14:14

We must all die; we are like water spilled on the ground, which cannot be gathered up again. But God will not take away life, and he devises means so that the banished one will not remain an outcast.

Conclusion

More important than isolated verses in the Bible is the entire testimony of the Bible. The Bible reveals a good and merciful God who is in the process of redeeming His rebellious creation and drawing it back to Himself. His will is to redeem and renew His entire creation. His love will not fail.

Ultimately, His desire to save all will be fulfilled, and He will reconcile the entire cosmos to Himself. This message is truly good news for every human being.

APPENDIX TWO
UNIVERSALIST THEOLOGY

In theology, Universalism is the doctrine that all mankind will finally attain salvation. Stated more fully, the beliefs which constitute the doctrine are: That God is; that his infinite power, wisdom and justice are modes of his essential nature, which is love; that he holds to mankind the relations of creator and father; that he is manifested through his works and providence; that he has disclosed through his highest creatures and especially through Jesus Christ, his character, will and purpose as to the duty and destiny of man; that he is continually working upon mankind through his cosmic and ethical forces, and by the operation of his Holy Spirit of truth, faith, hope and love; and that thus guided, disciplined, and inspired, all his children will eventually clear themselves from evil and achieve perfected character, with its resulting power, peace and joy, so that a complete moral harmony of the universe will be attained, and God will be all in all.

Man: Man is not under the wrath and curse of God for the sins of his ancestors; but he is under the difficulties and dangers of inherited and acquired defect and weakness; that his chief peril, the real, demonstrable hell into which he may fall is degeneration—the failure to live up to his organic capacity; that the evils which enmesh him are, however, challenges of his strength; that pain is the great stimulator of his energy—the prolonged birth-pang of his higher powers; and that his agonizing conflict with evil is only the fair price of perfected character and eternal life.

Universalism emphasizes the importance of faith in man as the highest organism of the visible creation and the chief visible work of God, and it contributes to the body of Christian doctrine this new article of faith: "We believe that man is created in the image of God, and is able to know and to do God's will." It is affirmed that man is not a fallen being, a worm, a slave, a wreck, but a developing being who began low down and is on his way up—not a ruin, but a mine, full of latent riches. His capacities are great, some of his actions are sublime; he is God's fellow-worker, coöperator, and agent. Through him chiefly, the divine purposes are wrought out on this earth. God furnishes the arena, the organism, the ever-renewed inspirations; but man does the work, and in doing it, he develops the one vital thing that God does not create, namely, character. Universalism affirms the spiritual unity of the race and the universality and ethical identity of all God's revelations to man.

Salvation: Universalists hold that moral development is not confined to this state of being, but is continuous with the whole duration of man: that salvation consists in the formation of a character conformed to God's will; that such character cannot be instantaneously acquired, nor produced in any other way than by the voluntary action of the individual; that rewards and punishments are not ends nor finalities, but aids to the development of character; that God's love is as clearly shown in penalty as in reward, since by the return of his deeds upon his own head, man is made aware that there is Somebody in the universe who cares which way he goes; that punishment is medicinal and corrective; that the remission of the natural penalties of voluntary transgression would be unmerciful; that forgiveness does not involve such remission, but works a change in the attitude of the soul which enables the transgressor to endure the consequences of his sin in such a way that they will ennoble instead of degrade him.

Universalism holds to the conversion of all bad beings into good beings. It discards the theory of endless punishments in favor of the doctrine of just punishments, which manifest a divine justice instead of an undivine vengeance. The Universalist protest is not against punishment, but against the endless continuance of sin and disobedience against everlasting anarchy in God's universe. The moral welfare of the universe requires that every moral being shall be brought into moral allegiance. Endless hell can no longer be held essential to the idea of God's justice; in fact, it would be a confession of God's failure, as though the Almighty should say, "I can not cure your sin, but I can torment you forever." Universalism holds that really divine action must be manifested by the conquering of wicked, not by the futile torture of the wicked.

Universalism affirms that the revelation of the divine character and purpose through Jesus Christ is the most potent generator of spiritual and ethical energy in the world; that the chief function of the church of Christ is to hold his ideal of life and character before men and help them to attain it; and that man can not find salvation by withdrawing from the sphere of life's appointed duties and activities, but that the great school of moral discipline and spiritual culture is to be found in the common personal relationships and ordinary pursuits of life.

The Bible: The Universalist Profession of Faith, adopted a century ago in this house, says: "We believe that the Holy Scriptures of the Old and New Testaments contain a revelation of the character of God, and of the duty, interest, and final destination of mankind."

It is held that the moral and spiritual content of the Bible constitute a progressive revelation adapted to the successive changes of man's development; that since a revelation must necessarily be intelligible to those to whom it is addressed, the Bible must be interpreted according to the present canons of historical criticism, and in the terms of man's present understanding and conscience; that it contains a record of man's spiritual experience and moral growth through many ages under the tuition of God's spirit, and that it stands pre-eminent in its power of communicating moral energy to the struggling souls of men.

Methods: It is held that all moral transformation and growth is from within outward; that the incarnation of God in Jesus Christ is representative of the method of the coming in of God's spirit in all men; that every soul is capable of receiving that spirit; that the entrance of the divine life into humanity is not an exceptional, official or magical act, but a process whose laws can be discovered and obeyed; that repentance of sin, the worship of God, obedience to the Christ, the service of men, the diligent discharge of duty, and the honoring of the common relationships of life, are all channels through which the soul may receive, in ever increasing measure, that divine energy which lifts it out of the power of sin and sorrow and forwards it on the way to perfection.

The Resurrection and the Future Life: It is held that the resurrection is experienced by each soul when, at the dissolution of the body, it enters upon a new order of existence. It is not conceived that death works any moral transformation, but that the soul enters the next state with the spiritual character which it has achieved on earth. It is believed that in the future life, all the opportunities for the further growth which the powers of the soul open to it will be accorded; that it will be there under the ministry of truth and love until truth and love have wrought within and upon it their perfect work.

—James M. Pullman, D.D.

From a 1903 lecture, "Exposition Of Universalism."

BIBLIOGRAPHY

Books

McVey, Steve. *52 Lies Heard in Church Every Sunday.*

Jersak, Bradley. *A More Christlike God.*

Ferguson, Everett. *Backgrounds of Early Christianity.*

McVey, Steve. *Beyond an Angry God.*

White, James R. *Drawn by the Father.*

Chan, Francis. *Erasing Hell.*

Mooney, Mick. *God's Grace Apart from Law.*

Sams, George W. *Heaven's Doors.*

Keathley, Don. *Hell's Illusion.*

Jersak, Bradley. *Her Gates Will Never Be Shut.*

Foret, Blaise. *It Is Finished.*

Smit, Robin. *It Is Finished.*

Kruger, C. Baxter. *Jesus and the Undoing of Adam.*

Giles, Keith. *Jesus Unbound.*

Giles, Keith. *Jesus Unexpected.*

Rabe, Andre. *Metanoia.*

Richards, Randolph, and J. O'Brien. *Misreading Scripture with Western Eyes.*

Bumfield, David. *Patristic Universalism.*

Wright, N. T. *Simply Jesus.*

Hart, David Bentley. *That All Shall Be Saved.*

Talbott, Thomas. *The Inescapable Love of God.*

Smith, Malcolm. *The Power of the Blood Covenant.*

Thayer, Thomas Baldwin. *Theology of Universalism.*

Keathley, Don. *Unhook the Book.*

Hanson, J. W. *Universalism: The Prevailing Doctrine of the Christian Church During the First Five Hundred Years.*

Internet

You can find the key words contained in the links below. If I were to give only the key words I used, you would be led to a large number of links. I have chosen to include only the links I actually read. In print, these will not appear as hyperlinks, but they can be located using the key words reflected in each link.

https://afkimel.wordpress.com/essential-readings-on-universalism/

https://salvationforall.org/7_History/2-catechetical_schools.html

https://en.wikipedia.org/wiki/History_of_Christian_universalism#cite_note-16

https://www.scribd.com/document/129064992/Apocatastasis-in-Patristic-Theology#

https://www.academia.edu/29436113/Meaning_of_the_word_apokatasta
  sis_in_Acts_3_21
https://www.patheos.com/blogs/unfundamentalistchristians/2017/04/indeed-
  many-universalism-early-church/
https://campuspress.yale.edu/keithderose/1129-2/#4
https://tentmaker.org/universalism.htm
https://godsplanforall.com/free-online-book/part-iii/chapter-21-calvinism-
  arminianism-and-universalism/
https://lambswar.blogspot.com/2011/03/is-universalism-heresy.html
https://jefffig.wordpress.com/tag/bible-verses-support-universalism/
https://christianuniversalist.org/articles/history-of-universalism/

ABOUT THE AUTHOR

Dale Hill, a product of the Jesus Movement, has been teaching the Bible for almost 60 years. He holds a BS in Communications and a Master of Theology.

His first book, *Basic Bible Doctrines*, has been used as a textbook for Bible classes in a Christian Middle School. He is also the author of *A Grace Primer*, an introduction to understanding the universal love, grace, and mercy of God from a biblical foundation.

ABOUT THE PUBLISHER

TWS Publishing curates more than books — we're shaping a heritage of scandalous grace. Every page we release points to this unshakable truth: *it is finished.*

Our olive branch logo reflects the Hebrew *etz shemen* — "tree of oil" — a symbol of anointing, sacred spaces, and the flame of God's presence made visible. Each book is part of a legacy that will keep bearing fruit for generations.

TWS
PUBLISHING

www.ingramcontent.com/pod-product-compliance
Lightning Source LLC
Chambersburg PA
CBHW062100080426
42734CB00012B/2705